BARRON'S

JOB HUNTING
FOR THE DISABLED

by

Edith Marks
Special Education Teacher
New York City Board of Education

Adele Lewis
Formerly President, Career Blazers Agency, Inc.
New York City

BARRON'S EDUCATIONAL SERIES, INC.
Woodbury, New York • London • Toronto • Sydney

To our very special friends and acquaintances whose
courage and determination made this book possible.

All inquiries should be addressed to:
Barron's Educational Series, Inc.
113 Crossways Park Drive
Woodbury, New York 11797

Library of Congress Catalog Card No. 82-22608

International Standard Book No. 0-8120-2487-7

Library of Congress Cataloging in Publication Data
Lewis, Adele Beatrice, 1927–
  Job hunting for the disabled.

  Includes bibliographies.
  1. Handicapped—Employment. 2. Job hunting.
I. Marks, Edith. II. Title.
HD7255.L48 1983   650.1′4′0880816   82-22608
ISBN 0-8120-2487-7

PRINTED IN THE UNITED STATES OF AMERICA

345   620   98765432

CONTENTS

PART III   ALTERNATIVES

Conclusion   211

APPENDIXES

INTRODUCTION

You're in the news almost daily. Authors use you as subjects for their award-winning books, plays and films. You're Terry Wiles playing yourself as a thalidomide victim in a TV dramatization. You're acting in *Children of a Lesser God*. You're a Vietnam veteran in *Coming Home*. Who are you? America's newest and one of its most vocal minorities—the disabled. You make up about 12 percent of the population, and your voice is being heard throughout the land as you vie for your place in work and leisure activities.

It's not always easy to reach that place. Not only do you have your own handicapping condition to contend with, but you have the attitudinal handicap of others who think you need the wrong kind of protection, such as institutionalization, or who are not persuaded that you can function, with technical help in some instances, accommodation in others, in the home, office or in play. Nevertheless, hidebound ideas of what an individual with a handicapping condition can or cannot do are rapidly dissolving in the wake of recent legislation stressing "affirmative action," and the determination of persons like yourself to reconstruct his or her own life.

We are all familiar with the great ones in history who, despite their handicapping conditions, achieved national and international recognition. Helen Keller, or course, comes immediately to mind, as does Franklin Delano Roosevelt, our thirty-second president, crippled with polio. It is now believed that both Albert Einstein and Abraham Lincoln suffered from handicapping conditions: Einstein from learning disabilities, Lincoln from depression. When Beethoven was profoundly deaf, he wrote his most sublime music. The late Nelson Rockefeller, former New York State governor, had dyslexia, a problem affecting his ability to read.

Today, however, there are countless of you who are unsung heroes, going quietly about your business. According to recent reports, there is not a business or profession from which you are excluded. Frances Koestler, in a pamphlet issued by the Public Affairs Committee, tells us about some of you who have made it, like Dr. Panzarella, whose body and limbs are paralyzed by multiple sclerosis. He has been director of one hospital, headed a rehabilitation clinic in another, served on the faculty of two community colleges, and was a professor at New York University's postgraduate medical school. Jim Sozoff, blind since the age of six, was chief of the U.S. Public Health Service's Community Health Aide Program for Alaska. Kay Beaty, deaf and blind, fitted with electronic aids to help her with paperwork, runs a food-vending stand. John J. Gavin, profoundly deaf, was director of international allergy research for Miles Laboratory in Elkhart, Indiana. Max Cleland, a triple Vietnam amputee, was elected to the Georgia State Senate, served on the U.S. Senate's Veterans Affairs staff, and was the administrator of the Veterans Administration.

In our personal and business lives we, too, have encountered individuals whose handicapping conditions hardly stood in the way of their pursuit of high goals. Our late optometrist, Dr. H. Rothman, was one such person. Stricken with polio as a young child, he went on, despite the dire predictions of his doctor, to walk, ride a bicycle, and put himself through optometry school. "Carolyn" is another. Although hampered by manic-depressive syndrome, Carolyn has managed to hold a job as a child-care worker. There are many Dr. Rothmans and Carolyns who make it in our society.

However, this book is dedicated to those of you who are ready, willing and able to step into the fast-flowing waters of the mainstream. How does one assess readiness, willingness, "ableness"? Let's look at each of these attributes.

Ready?

Perhaps one of the first things to realize is that everyone has a handicap. In the general population, these handicaps are often euphemistically called strengths and weaknesses. Some of our strengths are clearly visible to others and, of course, to ourselves. We may excel in sports, academic skills, gardening, cooking, organizational work or business affairs. The extent and variety of our strengths are reflected in the myriad of professions, jobs and hobbies that we perform.

Our weaknesses, on the other hand, are often looked upon as an inability to perform or learn, possibly an incompetence in one or more areas. It is not surprising, then, when we tote up our personal balance sheet, that we place our strengths on the credit side and our weaknesses on the debit side of our personal ledger. Yet our innate struggle to overcome a particular weakness or disability is often the stuff of our success, an asset not to be overlooked. Readiness, therefore, is the ability to assess carefully our strengths and weaknesses, plumb our own depths for resources and come up with a mind-set to pursue a realistic and obtainable goal.

Willing?

As with readiness, willingness implies that we assess our strengths and weaknesses, but in combination with our psychological strengths. It is the psychological strength that fuels the desire to overcome whatever obstacle blocks the path to achievement—a strengthening of resolve to obtain a certificate, a diploma, a college degree, or to get a particular job teams up with those inherent aptitudes and abilities. Willingness is also an openness to consider a number of different possibilities whether in training, education or job opportunities. Willingness is the ability to delay gratification in the interests of a long-range goal.

Able?

As we indicated in our opening paragraphs, you as a disabled individual are not normally excluded from jobs or professions, provided you have the skills. Those of you with whom we have spoken take care to emphasize the *able* in disabled. The marketplace, since the advent of affirmative action, is more open to you than ever before. However, you cannot expect to compete without possessing specific training and expertise. Adjustment of the environment through "reasonable accommodation" is written into the law, and must accordingly be afforded, provided you have the skills to do the job.

Ready, willing and able thus implies both a mind-set and skills acquisition that allows you to participate in the world of work. In this book, we will be discussing how you can become a functioning member of the mainstream and a productive, contributing member of society.

Acknowledgments

We would like to acknowledge the contributions and assistance we received from the following individuals and members of organizations serving persons with disabilities. John C. Deely and the staff at the Institute for the Crippled and Disabled; Alfred B. Miller and staff of the Federation Employment and Guidance Services; Joseph Palevsky and staff of the Office of Vocational Services, New York City; the staff at the Mayor's Office of the Handicapped, New York City; Alison Alcolay and staff at Just One Break; Curtis Brewer and staff of Untapped Resources, Inc.; Joe Parriot and staff of the Margaret Gate Institute; Rami Rabby, author of *Locating, Recruiting and Hiring the Disabled,* and staff at the New York Association for the Blind.

We also wish to acknowledge with deep appreciation the sharing of their personal experiences of the individuals highlighted in this book: Paul Sottnek, Theresa Stratthaus, Gregory Murakiewicz, Linda Slone and Patricia Karlsen. And lastly, we wish to thank Jason Marks for his invaluable editorial assistance.

PART I

THE JOB SITUATION

1

THE WORKING WORLD

Where do you fit in? If you are just starting out, recently rehabilitated, changing jobs in midlife, changing careers or returning to work after a long hiatus, the job outlook can be a frightening prospect. The first thought that may enter your mind is that although there seem to be plenty of jobs out there, the job that will suit you doesn't exist. The second thought is the sobering realization that your condition may somehow handicap you from getting the job you covet. Both of these assumptions, fortunately, have been proved false, since a goodly number of persons with handicapping conditions are working in all levels of industry and services. Granted that equal status with the general population is still a dream. The statistics tell us that less than half of you are in the working force as of the 1970 census. Although there have certainly been some gains over the past ten years as a result of the Rehabilitation Act of 1973, one still comes across the sentiment that these depressed figures will be difficult to change. However, is this thinking realistic? The Directory of Occupational Titles lists over twenty thousand job titles that exist in this country. It is estimated that over two million new (never held before) jobs open each year. Added to this number, the average worker changes jobs or careers three to five times in his or her working life. Each time a change is made, the job is added to the pool. Jobs, then, do exist. Success in finding a job, it would appear, involves learning to "read" the market and to hone your skills and abilities to take advantage of that market.

The Job Market

Let's take a look at this market. Fluctuations may be connected to any number of national and international events. The President and Congress might declare tighter money credit, a policy that will discourage business expansion, and that ultimately results in a decrease in jobs in certain industries. Increases in city and states taxes in one locality may force some companies to seek areas where the rate of taxation is more attractive, causing a shift of jobs from one location to another. International events may lead to mutual muscle-flexing among the superpowers, followed by an increase in defense spending, leading to a greater demand for engineers and technicians. Outcry about environmental problems, educational failure, decay of cities may generate funding sources for studying and alleviating these problems.

With every change in technology new jobs open, just as changes in society create new kinds of jobs. The high crime rate has been responsible for an upswing in the burglar alarm security systems. One of the largest companies in the field, Pinkerton, Inc., reports that it has added more than six thousand people to its staff during the past several years. Companies that connect burglar alarms to police stations are springing up all over the country, creating a source of new jobs.

Today, small businesses as well as large corporations conduct their accounting procedures—payrolls, billing, inventory control—with the help of computer technology. As a result, a person trained in the use of computers will have little difficulty finding a choice position. Mary P., a computer-trained technician, recently lost her arm. After undergoing rehabilitation, she had absolutely no difficulty securing a job. In fact, her placement officer at her vocational rehabilitation center was amazed at the rapidity with which she was hired.

Pollution control is another industry wherein growth is continuous. Never has the public been so aware of the dangers of hazardous waste materials. The recent tragedies of Love Canal and the Three Mile Island nuclear near-accident have created a public demand that attention be paid to environmental factors. This consciousness of the environment on the part of the public and private sectors has stimulated jobs with industries that manufacture these materials, and a new breed of job titles, that of environmentalists and ecologists who act as watchdogs over the use of our land and resources.

Domestic affairs also contribute to flux in the job market. If individuals perceive that shoe repair is more costly than buying a new pair of shoes, the demand for shoe repairmen diminishes. In the 1970s, this actually happened. During that period, however, there was a growth in the number of new homes being constructed, increasing the demand for carpenters and other home-building services.

Flux, of course, is inevitable, but there is one stable element. The same events that cause changes in international and national affairs eventually create new jobs—jobs that will need people who are trained to carry out new or revised job objectives. Job prospects, therefore, according to the U.S. Department of Labor, Division of Occupational Outlook, are good. Employment is expected to increase in almost all occupations throughout the 1980s, provided that past trends continue, that there will be no war, that unemployment will not exceed a specific level, and that our system of government and basic social values do not change.

Where the Opportunities Are

The U.S. Department of Labor issues a number of publications that give both present and projected job prospects. *The Job Outlook in Brief,* for example, lists those jobs that will show the fastest growth through the 1990s. These include: bank clerks, bank officers, financial managers, business machine repairers, city managers, computer service technicians, construction in-

spectors, dental assistants, dental hygienists, dining room attendants, dishwashers, flight attendants, guards, health service
administrators, homemaker-home health aides, industrial machinery repairers, landscape architects, licensed practical
nurses, nursing aides, lithographers, orderlies and attendants,
occupational therapists, occupational therapy assistants, respiratory therapy workers, teacher aides. Table 1 will give you an
idea of the number of annual openings in each of these fast-
growing fields. Note, however, that although some jobs are
growing rapidly, the number of openings is still relatively small.
Thus, if you choose to become a travel agent rather than a bank
clerk (nineteen hundred travel agents needed, forty-five thousand bank clerks needed), your chances of getting a job as a
bank clerk are twenty-five times greater than your chances of
obtaining a job as a travel agent. Some of these prospects are
changing rapidly, however. Only five thousand respiratory workers are listed in the *Job Outlook.* Yet a recent article in the *New
York Times* indicated that there is now a critical shortage of
workers in this field. Job opportunities throughout the country
for experienced respiratory workers far exceed the number of
qualified personnel.

Other fields that have not made the Department of Labor's
most-wanted list appear, in the market at large, to be causing
more than a ripple. Traffic manager jobs are now going for high
salaries. With the cost of moving materials increasing, the value
of the traffic manager increases. He or she is the person who is
involved with cost effectiveness, customer service and inventory
deployment—critical keys to profitability. The baking industry,
whose sales are put at more than $15 billion a year, constantly
needs workers who are trained in baking science. By 1985, it is
estimated, a billion tons of coal will be dug out. That figure means
jobs in the coal industry. Paramedic and paralegal positions continue to proliferate as doctors and lawyers find that routine medical care and legal tasks can be handled by trained technicians.
Engineering technicians can apply their talents to a variety of
fields ranging from the repair of robots to product safety. Specialized skills in fields as diverse as sailboat building, zoo work,
catfish farming, and glass blowing are all part of the greater job

FASTEST GROWING JOBS, 1978–90

OCCUPATION	ANNUAL OPENINGS
Bank Clerks	45,000
Bank officers and financial managers	28,000
Business machine repairers	4,200
City managers	350
Computer service technicians	5,400
Construction inspectors	2,200
Dental assistants	11,000
Dental hygienists	6,000
Dining room attendants and dishwashers	37,000
Flight attendants	4,800
Guards	70,000
Health service administrators	18,000
Homemaker-home health aides	36,000
Industrial machinery repairers	58,000
Landscape architects	1,100
Licensed practical nurses	60,000
Lithographers	2,300
Nursing aides, orderlies, and attendants	94,000
Occupational therapists	2,500
Occupational therapy assistants	1,100
Physical therapists	2,700
Podiatrists	600
Respiratory therapy workers	5,000
Speech pathologists and audiologists	3,900
Teacher aides	26,000
Travel agents	1,900

Note: For these occupations, employment in 1990 is projected to be at least 50 percent higher than it was in 1978.

Source: "The Job Outlook in Brief," reprint from *Occupational Outlook Quarterly*. Washington, D.C.: U.S. Department of Labor, Spring 1980.

picture. Thus, it is advisable to use the information from the Department of Labor as a guide to job searching, but to remain open to the many interesting and unusual occupations that exist.

A second method for examining the job market is to determine those jobs that are likely to be most available in the 1990s. An analysis of Table 2 below tells us that secretaries and stenographers head the list. Even with the advent of the new office technology, the need for competent office help remains steady. The high number of retail workers indicates that although tech-

JOBS WITH THE MOST OPENINGS, 1978–90

OCCUPATION	ANNUAL OPENINGS
Secretaries and stenographers	305,000
Retail sales workers	226,000
Building custodians	180,000
Cashiers	119,000
Bookkeeping workers	96,000
Nursing aides, orderlies, and attendants	94,000
Cooks and chefs	86,000
Kindergarten and elementary teachers	86,000
Registered nurses	85,000
Assemblers	77,000
Waiters and waitresses	70,000
Guards	70,000
Blue-collar worker supervisors	69,000
Local truck drivers	64,000
Accountants	61,000
Licensed practical nurses	60,000
Typists	59,000
Carpenters	58,000
Industrial machinery repairers	58,000
Real estate agents and brokers	50,000
Construction laborers	49,000
Engineers	46,500
Bank clerks	45,000
Private household workers	45,000
Receptionists	41,000
Wholesale trade sales workers	40,000

Note: Replacement needs and growth are projected to cause these occupations to offer the largest numbers of openings. Competition for openings will vary by occupation.

Source: "The Job Outlook in Brief," reprint from *Occupational Outlook Quarterly.* Washington, D.C.: U.S. Department of Labor, Spring 1980.

nology may be working to aid the retailer, it is certainly not replacing personnel. In the educational field, kindergarten and elementary teachers comprise many of the job openings. Although this figure is not broken down into specialties, the passage of the Education of the Handicapped Act, Public Law 94-142, and the Vocational Education Acts has increased the demand for teachers trained in special and vocational education. If we reexamine the fastest-growing jobs, we find that computer service technicians are listed in this grouping, but the number of annual openings is too small to appear in the "jobs with the most openings." Yet our experience at the Agency belies this information. Computer technicians are in demand. A recent development has also turned the engineering market around; engineering graduates are now on the most-wanted list for company recruiters. Offers for newly graduated engineers spiralled to $30,000 per annum. What appears to be occurring is that large companies anticipating an upturn in the economy are again preparing to expand.

There are also a goodly number of jobs largely unaffected by changing times. These are jobs where skills can be transferred from one industry to another. We noted that secretaries and stenographers headed the list of "jobs with the most openings." The reason for this is clear. A secretary, steno, or typist can work with an engineer, doctor, lawyer, accountant—in any business with little or no additional training. A bookkeeper or accountant has little difficulty moving from one industry to another. A computer technician can program information from a variety of services into a terminal. In short, many of the skilled office jobs can be transferred from one industry to another. This fact is responsible for the steady availability of office personnel openings.

Retail workers, building custodians, cashiers, cooks and chefs, assemblers, waiters and waitresses, guards, truck drivers, household workers are also in demand, and for the same reasons. These jobs can fit easily into a number of different businesses and services.

The helping professions as well experience much the same latitude. However, movement from state to state is somewhat limited due to state licensing requirements.

It is important to bear in mind that the figures promulgated by the Department of Labor may not reflect the actual job openings in your area. You might want to take advantage of another of the publications issued by the department, *Occupations in Demand at Job Service Offices*. This monthly publication prints out jobs, openings available for the month, openings still available at the end of the month, pay range and areas that have the most significant number of openings. A close reading of this material will help you to assess the kinds of jobs available to you in your area.

If you plan to purchase *The Job Outlook in Brief,* you can send for it to the Consumer Information Center, Department B, Pueblo, Colorado 81009. The cost is $2.75. You may wish to examine all possibilities in greater depth. This information can be found in the *Occupational Outlook Handbook,* which can be purchased for $8.00 from a regional office of the Bureau of Labor Statistics. It is also usually available in libraries and offices of guidance and employment counselors.

2

TAKE A PERSONAL INVENTORY

We are happiest when we work in fields and situations where we feel most comfortable. If we are fortunate, those fields will become evident early enough in our lives for us to direct our energies immediately toward our chosen objectives. Generally, however, career choice for many of us is serendipitous. Chances are we may not even have clear goals formulated when we graduate from school. Vague notions of ideal jobs hover gently in our heads. As with our notion of the ideal mate, we tell ourselves that we'll know the perfect job when we see it. For some of us that perfect job never materializes, while for others each job contains interesting and exciting aspects that make it worthwhile. Much of what happens on a job, our ultimate choice of job or career, and our affinity for that career depend on what we bring to it in terms of skills, attitudes and personality characteristics.

In our many years of employment service, we have been able to assist people in choosing certain kinds of jobs and/or fields that appear to be most suited to their skills and personalities. Informally, we have discussed those skills, hobbies, preferred working conditions and personality characteristics of our clients that have helped us to match their job specifications to their individual needs and aspirations. To enable you to better understand how your characteristics, skills, interests and needs can help you to choose the most suitable job, we have prepared three informal inventories: Experience/Interest Inventory; Personality Profile; Working Conditions Inventory. Spend some time with these inventories. They may help you pinpoint your job direction.

Experience/Interest Inventory

This inventory will help you establish those skills and activities you enjoy and that are marketable. These skills and activities can be added to your resume. Be sure to consider hobbies, volunteer work and paid experience.

Clerical

Have you had experience or are you interested in any of the following?

Typing: letters, forms, lists, envelopes

Writing: envelopes, keeping records

Sorting: mail, papers, books, materials

Filing: letters, forms, catalogues

Answering telephones: switchboards, other systems

Office machines: calculator, adding machine, typewriter, word processor, etc.

Office equipment: copying machines, Xerox, addressograph, multilith, ditto, mimeograph, etc.

Greeting visitors

Collecting money

Other _____

_____

_____

Experience in clerical work covers all fields. You already have a handle on gaining a job of your choice.

Clerical/Numerical

Have you had experience or are you interested in the following?

Making change
Writing receipts
Keeping work records
Entering accounts
Adding columns of figures
Working on payroll
Working with calculator or adding machine
Other _____
_____
_____

Experience in the numerical end of clerical work also covers every field. Interest in the field will probably govern your choice of job.

Spatial Ability

Have you had experience or are you good at the following?

Drawing
Blueprint reading
Map reading
Other _____
_____

Can you use any of the following tools?

Compass
T-square

Triangle

Other _____

_____

Fields open to persons with good spatial abilities include engineering, architecture, cartography, publishing, medical and technical journals, encyclopedias. You may also consider becoming a draftsman/woman where you will be trained to execute ideas and designs developed by engineers and architects.

Sales

Have you had sales experience or are you interested in any of the following areas?

Via the telephone

Door-to-door in your neighborhood

Cosmetics

Groceries

Boutique items

At street fairs

At flea markets

In a department store

Fast foods

Lemonade when a child

Other _____

_____

_____

_____

Experience or enjoyment in selling is another skill that covers all fields. Selling is integral to the functioning of every business. If you've got the skill and desire, use it.

Services

Have you had experience in or are you interested in any of these activities?

Caring: for babies, baby sitting, for young children, teacher's assistant, for older people, for sick people

Cooking: your own meals, meals for others, in a restaurant

Baking: pastry, bread, cookies

Cleaning: your own home, for others—dusting, polishing, washing clothes, ironing, washing walls and windows, washing cars

Shopping: your own, for others, for a restaurant

Grooming: cutting and washing hair, manicuring, massaging, shaving

Helping: in a restaurant—cleaning, serving, cooking, dishwashing
in a hotel—laundry, cleaning rooms, making beds, room service, busboy/girl

Gardening: your own, other people's, mowing lawns, raking, weeding, harvesting fruits and vegetables

Teaching: students, at camp, older people

Volunteering: for cleanup drivers, clubs, fund-raising

Other _____
_____
_____
_____

Service jobs cover an extremely wide range of fields and occupations. You may choose to turn your experience and interest into a professional occupation such as that of social worker, nurse, teacher, dietician or psychologist, or consider any of the health-related technical fields. Or you may elect the middle-management, skilled, semiskilled or unskilled route. Depending upon the level of training, for example, your interest in cooking and baking can lead you into such occupations as dietician, chef, restaurateur, food manager, hostess, host, waiter or waitress. Cleaning can escalate into a number of occupations and trades, ranging from laundry work to office maintenance. Your shopping skills may develop into various types of merchandising jobs. Gardening skills can be transformed into landscaping and nursery careers. Interest in grooming naturally falls into areas of cosmetology and barbering.

Mechanical/Skills

Have you had experience or are you interested in any of the following?

Driving shift cars, automatic transmission, motorcycles, boats, tractors, trucks, etc.

Operating snow plows, fork lifts, farm equipment

Operating movie cameras, slide projectors, film projectors, tape recorders

Operating electric drills, saws, hammers, pneumatic drills, welders

Other _____

_____

_____

_____

Mechanical/Repairing/Building

Have you had experience or are you interested in repairing or building any of the following?

Bicycles, tricycles

Broken toys

Radios, tape recorders, television

Toasters, fans, blenders, mixers

Washing machines, refrigerators, vacuum cleaners, stoves

Motors in cars, boats, etc.

Damaged cars—fenders, body work

Home repairs:
  Plastering
  Painting
  Wallpapering
  Plumbing
  Electrical work

Hi-fi equipment

Cabinets

Models

Houses

Furniture

Boats

Other _____

_____

_____

_____

You are fortunate. Mechanical skills and interest can lead to a great many jobs in the trade and technical areas. The majority of jobs in industry depend upon persons who have one or more of these kinds of skills. Fields such as construction, building trades, printing, transportation or driving occupations could not exist if it were not for workers with mechanical skills. Within each industry, there is also usually a department devoted exclusively to the repair of items used or produced by that industry. Competent repairers and mechanics are a unique and select breed, and are perhaps among the most sought-after employees by companies and organizations. In addition, if you have a wide range of skills, you might even consider going into business for yourself. Many a "fix-it" shop has grown from a one-person organization into a major business.

Creative

Have you had experience or are you interested in any of the following?

   Singing or dancing in a show

   Playing a musical instrument

   Acting

   Working in stage production, such as costume and set designing

   Sewing your own clothes, clothes for others, needlework

   Writing books, stories, poetry, articles

   Weaving rugs, belts, blankets

   Knitting, crocheting

   Working in pottery, ceramics

   Drawing, painting, sculpting

   Designing posters, clothes, sets

   Photography

   Other _____

   _____

   _____

   _____

There are a number of jobs and fields where creativity and talent are considered an asset. You might want to look into journalism, public relations, advertising, theater, foundations, museums, television and radio, communications. Your experience with handicrafts can lead to jobs with boutiques, to designing or to opening your own business.

Personality Profile

Generally the kind of job offered to you is based on the image you project. For example, if you prefer a job that involves meeting or working with groups of people, your most positive personality characteristics for success at this job would be amiability, energy, consideration, modesty, poise, dignity, good organization and politeness. Certain jobs and fields also project images. Which adjectives come to mind when you think about yourself? Which adjectives come to mind when you think teaching, acting, working in a factory?

To help you evaluate some of your own personality traits, we have prepared a short checklist. Simply circle those qualities that seem to represent you. In addition ask a friend or relative to choose the characteristics that best describe you. Analyze both sets of responses. You may be pleasantly surprised at what others see in you, as was one of the authors of this book who, when she was first looking for a job, was amazed to find that prospective employers considered her poised, an attribute she had never ascribed to herself.

When you have completed the checklist, analyze your responses in relation to the description of characteristics that are found in a number of fields.

agreeable	energetic	kindly	sensitive
alert	exacting	lazy	serious
bold	fair	literate	sharp
businesslike	flippant	mercurial	shrewd
cautious	forceful	orderly	shy
close-mouthed	frank	patient	steady
competitive	gentle	peevish	strong
confident	gracious	polished	suspicious
cool	hasty	powerful	tactful
creative	honest	punctual	unassuming
deliberate	humorous	quiet	unpretentious
determined	impatient	reliable	urbane
diplomatic	impulsive	reserved	virtuous
discreet	informal	resourceful	wary
dreamy	irritable	restless	well-adjusted
elegant	jolly	self-possessed	well-bred

If you have personality traits that fall into the grouping of *agreeable, diplomatic, businesslike, orderly, resourceful, self-possessed, strong, serious, tactful, unassuming, well-adjusted, punctual* and *well-bred*, you will fit into almost every kind of job or profession. Along with the above traits, you might also find that you've checked off traits that cluster around such characteristics as *competitive, forceful, creative, bold, powerful*. These characteristics would be ideal for jobs in marketing, sales, advertising, public relations, securities. If you find that your traits are tilting toward the *quiet, gentle, orderly, serious, steady, patient, sedate, literate, sensitive, discreet*, you might want to investigate jobs with libraries, education, or many of the clerical or semiskilled jobs such as accounting, bookkeeping, computer, lab technician work or copyediting. At the other extreme, your personality may really percolate when you are involved with people exhibiting traits of elegance, jollity, graciousness, polish, confidence. Here you may succeed in public relations, advertising, college and high school teaching, journalism, theater, sales, small business, retailing, service-oriented jobs and the entire field of communications.

You have probably noted that a number of what could be termed negative characteristics are listed in this informal inventory. Although you cannot be expected to shine each day and be accommodating to every situation, traits such as *peevishness, impatience, restlessness, suspiciousness, irritability, flippancy, laziness* tend to work against you in the job world. If you find yourself checking more than five of these characteristics, you might consider discussing these feelings with a counselor.

Working Conditions Inventory

Working conditions is the third category you will want to consider. No doubt you will have preferences. Examine the working conditions listed. Then compare your response with the analysis of responses.

1. *People, Things, Ideas*

    (a) I really enjoy working with people in any capacity. I'm the kind of person who likes spending evenings with friends and acquaintances.

    (b) I prefer working with things or ideas. I am happy spending evenings alone or on projects such as sewing, building models, doing craft work, writing, painting, etc.

    (c) I enjoy activities where I can figure things out, plan ahead.

    (d) I like to persuade people to do things my way.

2. *Ideals, Beliefs*

    (a) I believe in the pursuit of money as an end in itself.

    (b) I believe that my work should somehow contribute to the betterment of society.

3. *Tempo, Variation*

    (a) I work best when faced with pressure and insurmountable odds.

    (b) I work best in a steady, evenly paced environment.

    (c) I like to do the same things every day.

    (d) I need a variety of things to do.

4. *Self-starter, Direction Taker*

    (a) I enjoy initiating activities, giving directions, whether it's at work, at parties or in the home.

    (b) I would rather listen quietly, wait for others to give directions.

    (c) Close supervision makes me nervous.

    (d) I'm uncomfortable when I have to make my own decisions.

5. *Creativity, Facts, Things*

    (a) I want to work with measurable facts, data, records, things.

    (b) I want to create, synthesize, innovate.

6. *Location, Activity*

    (a) I prefer restricted areas such as an office, lab, classroom.

    (b) I shudder at the idea of being hemmed in. I need to work in open space most of the time.

    (c) I like a job where I'm required to move around a lot.

    (d) I prefer a job where I can stay put.

7. *Size of Company*

    (a) I like a small organization where I can do everything and where I can learn about everything.

    (b) I like a medium-sized company, big enough for benefits, but not so big that I'll get lost in the shuffle.

    (c) I want to work in a giant company. I feel more secure that way.

An Analysis of Your Responses

If you answered (a) to *Question #1*, the following jobs or fields might be most suitable for you:

Administration

Barbering

Bartending

Buying

Cashiering

City managing

Claims representative

Clergy

Collection

Cosmetology

Counseling

Credit managing

Driving (public transportation)

FBI

Firefighting

Flight attending

Funeral directing, embalming

Guarding

Homemaking

Hotel housekeeping and assisting

Hotel management

Insurance

Libraries

Mail carrying

Modeling

Personnel recruitment

Police work

Public relations

Purchasing

Real estate

Reception

Reservation, ticketing and passenger agent

Reporting

Selling

Signal department workers

Teaching

Teaching aide

Urban planning

If you answered (b), the following jobs or fields might be most appropriate:

Accounting, bookkeeping

Air transportation (air traffic controller, mechanic, etc.)
Clerical
Cleaning and related occupations
Computer and related occupations
Conservation occupations
Construction
Copy editing
Design
Drafting
Engineering
Environmental science
Food service preparation
Foundry work
Industrial production and related occupations
Insurance underwriting
Laboratory technician
Library science occupations
Machine operator
Math, statistics
Mechanic and repairer
Physical science
Printing
Railroad occupations
Typist

If you answered (c), you might want to look into the following jobs or fields:

Administration
Computer and related occupations
Conservation occupations

Copy editing
Engineering
Environmental sciences
Industrial production
Insurance
Law
Librarians
Library technician and assistant
Real estate agent and broker
Teaching
Travel agenting
Transportation

If you answered (d), try out the following fields or jobs:

Administration
Clergy
Counseling occupations
Fundraising
Hotel housekeeping and assisting
Legal services
Public relations
Purchasing agent
Teaching

Question #2 defines goals based on conviction. Some persons choose careers wherein the primary focus is on financial gain. Others prefer to place interest first and sacrifice high remuneration for a job where they feel they contribute to society. In some cases a few lucky individuals are able to combine the ideal job with a high-income-producing position. Whatever direction you take, it is important to remember that the choice is based on your interests and desires. If it is what you want to do, it's right for you.

By and large, those of you who responded to (a) should consider those organizations primarily involved in profit making. Some of these organizations include:

All business

Advertising

Construction

Insurance and credit

Investment and banking

International trade

Manufacturing

Printing

Sales

Transportation

Where contribution to the betterment of society is the primary consideration, the following fields would probably be more acceptable to you:

Communications and related fields

Clergy, rabbinate

Environmental science

Life science

*Medical occupations

Nursing occupations

Performing arts

Physical sciences

Social sciences

* Among the lucky few who can combine high income with love of work.

Social services

Teaching and related occupations

Therapy and rehabilitation

Question #3 poses an interesting problem. It involves both pressure and variety. At times these terms are synonymous. Pressure itself is an interesting concept. What may be a high-pressure job in New York will be low pressure in Oshkosh. Pressure may be caused by an erratic manager, inadequate management or outside forces, or may, indeed, be a function of the job. Those jobs wherein pressure seems to fuel the operation (a) include:

Administration

Advertising

Air traffic control

Book and magazine publishing

Drivers of public vehicles

Employment agencies

Inner-city teaching

Interior decorating

Newspapers

Nursing

Public relations

Printing

Tax accountancy

Temporary services

The arts, TV, films, music

Generally speaking, the steady-paced jobs (b) can be found in areas such as:

Clerical occupations

Computer and related occupations

Finance, banking
Industrial production
Insurance occupations
Library science
Machine occupations
The sciences

Jobs that fall into the category of repetitive work (c) include:

Factory work
Clerical work
Cashiering
Machine operating
Sales of one product

Jobs with variety (d) include those found in:

Advertising
Administration
The Arts
Employment agencies
Repairing
Journalism
Public relations
Publishing
Teaching
Temporary services
Service industries

Question #4 probes leadership qualities. You may enjoy the leadership roles of taking responsibility, running the show, or you may prefer to be a team member of an organization, taking direction from a capable leader. If you marked (a) and (c) you would probably be happiest in positions that tap your initiative, such as:

Administrative

Advertising

Clergy

Communications and related occupations

Education and related fields

Performing arts

Personnel

Publishing

Public relations

Sales

Science research

If you marked (b) and (d) you prefer those organizations where teamwork is essential. Of course, leadership and initiative are also essential in these fields, but persons with these qualities usually become the managers and supervisors.

City, state and federal jobs

Construction occupations

Industrial production

Health occupations

Mechanics and repairers

Office occupations

Service occupations

Scientific and technical operations

Social service occupations

Transportation occupations

Question #5 ascertains how comfortable you are working with concrete objects or abstract ideas. If you answered (a), the fields or jobs that would probably be most attractive to you would be in:

Accounting, bookkeeping

Health and human services

Factory work

Industrial work

Math, statistics

Mechanics, repairs

Office work

Research

The sciences

If your answer was (b), you should probably seek work in fields such as:

Administration

Advertising

Analysis (labor, Wall Street, etc.)

Films

Public relations

Publishing

Teaching (high school, college)

Television

Question #6 addresses the problem of environment. Some of you may enjoy or tolerate well working in a confined space. Others may feel hemmed in by walls, time clocks, schedules, imposed deadlines. Since the majority of fields have definite space allocations, we are not listing them individually, but suggest rather that when you explore the job market, you consider how much confinement is amenable to you. For those of you who are unalterably opposed to working in a closed-in area, several fields offer possibilities:

Athletics

Archaeology

Construction

Conservation occupations

Door-to-door sales

Driving occupations

Forestry

Geology

Landscape architecture

Performing arts

Rangers

Uniformed services

Pest control

Question #7 is basically a matter of preference. When you are contemplating the pros and cons of a job, consider whether it meets your needs with respect to size. In this instance, however, we suggest flexibility. Policies differ from company to company. A small concern may have as many benefits and as much security as a larger organization. A large organization may develop the diseases of bureaucracy. A very small organization may be short of capital. Carefully examine all the alternatives. Try to avoid generalizations and make an educated decision based on facts rather than bias.

Admittedly, these inventories merely brush the surface of the occupations that are available to you. For finer tuning of your aptitudes, strengths and weaknesses, you may want to take some of the published inventories. Your vocational counselor, either state, private or veteran, is in a position to administer a comprehensive aptitude test. There are even tests that do not require the use of paper and pencil, substituting instead a demonstration of how well you can perform the job. One of these tests is called the micro-tower.

Or you might want to check yourself out on a variety of work-inventory scales. You can find books on mechanical aptitude and spatial relationships in your public library.

Another source for matching skills to jobs can be found in one of the Department of Labor's publications. The fall 1978 issue of *Occupational Outlook Quarterly,* for example, lists a number of fields that include: industrial production and related occupations, office occupations, service occupations, education and related occupations, sales, construction, transportation, scientific and technical occupations, mechanics and repairers, health, social science jobs, social services, art, design, and communications-related occupations. They have also developed twenty-three characteristics that include: high school, technical school or apprenticeship training, junior college, college; problem-solving ability; use of tools or machinery; instructing of others, repetitious, hazardous, outdoors, physical stamina, generally confined, precision, work with detail, frequent public contact, part-time, able to see results, creativity, influence others, competition on the job, work as part of a team, jobs widely scattered and initiative. Obviously this list combines several categories of attributes: extent of formal education, manual skills, personal characteristics, characteristics of specific jobs and environmental concerns. These characteristics are arranged in a chart alongside the various occupational titles, enabling you to determine which characteristics are most likely to be found within each occupational cluster.

For example, an automobile painter would perceive through the use of this chart that training would be available for the most part through unions and employers; that a high school diploma may or may not be required; that the job specs call for the use of tools and machinery, that the job is hazardous, that an individual needs to have physical stamina, that work is in a generally confined space and requires precision, and that jobs are widely scattered.

A kindergarten or elementary school teacher would need to have graduated from college, have problem-solving abilities, the ability to instruct others and be able to work with detail; enjoy frequent public contact, be creative, be able to influence others, work as part of a team, possess initiative and know that the jobs are widely scattered.

If you are just entering the job market, or are about to change your career, it can be both instructive and rewarding to send for a copy of this reprint from the *Occupational Outlook Quarterly*. A second publication that may be helpful is the *Occupational Outlook Handbook*, which lists about twenty thousand job titles. You can purchase these publications directly from the Department of Labor, Bureau of Labor Statistics, Washington, D.C. 20210, or you can use them in your public or school libraries.

CURTIS BREWER

"If one thinks a disability is a negative, then it negates the person." Curtis Brewer is not a man to be negated. Recipient in 1980 of the President's Trophy as Handicapped American of the Year (1979) Brewer merely looks upon this honor as a means for helping other individuals with disabilities to rise above their handicapping conditions.

Brewer's story is a remarkable study of a courageous and determined man. Stricken with transverse myelitis, a spinal cord inflammation of unknown origin, Curtis Brewer, from 1955 on, found himself becoming increasingly disabled. Today he is a quadraplegic requiring a respirator for breathing assistance. He cannot perform any physical act for himself and needs the constant attention of aides. Yet his physical disability has in no way diminished his spirit or blocked his attainments. In 1956 he was graduated from the New School for Social Research with a B.A. He studied at New York University's School of Public Administration and Social Services. His formal education might have stopped there except for the fact that his work was now taking a legalistic turn. He therefore enrolled in the Brooklyn Law School and in 1974 was granted his J.D. degree.

Curtis Brewer's work grew out of his efforts as a private ombudsman—assisting individuals to cut governmental red tape. From this work, Brewer perceived the need for a more structured organization. Thus, Untapped Resources, Inc. was born. Untapped Resources, Inc. mirrors Brewer's own commitment to seeking the most expedient solution to a problem. It provides comprehensive legal services for the physically handicapped. The success of this organization is reflected in the number of cases Brewer has successfully argued. He has won over 98 percent of them. Yet Brewer introduces nothing new. He simply works with existing laws, laws that without Brewer's incentive might have been summarily dismissed or at best ignored.

Brewer doesn't retreat and glumly watch a system fail. He attacks the system with its own tools, using these tools to rebuild the corrosive effect of time and misuse. Untapped Resources, Inc. is Brewer's instrument with which he unsnarls bureaucratic red tape. The legal services provided by this organization to physically or orthopedically disabled individuals covers a wide variety of problems. Brewer sees it as his mission to help individuals solve these problems.

To keep the organization afloat, Brewer engages in fundraising, lecturing, writing and public advocacy. Whether he functions from behind a desk or propped up in bed, he is actively engaged in developing methods for solving old and new problems.

"Normal is as normal does," Brewer replies to a question about his wife and son. His son is on scholarship in a Ph.D. program and his wife works at a university. Nevertheless, Curtis Brewer is proud to add that he considers the major responsibility of the household to be his and has always taken an active role in household affairs.

Talking with Curtis Brewer, one is struck by the breadth of his understanding and commitment, qualities that run like a vein through all of his activities. When, as administrator of a neuropsychological research laboratory, he became involved in a pioneering system that would enable him to operate his wheelchair and other electrical appliances from a switch mounted in front of his chin and operated by pressure from his tongue, his requirements became the prototype for a commercial model. Another first involved the cooperation of the New York Telephone Company, which fitted specialized equipment in the form of an ear plug fitted to a pair of glasses and a switch apparatus. With a touch of his tongue on the switch, Brewer and other individuals with similar problems can summon an operator who will dial the number.

What advice does Brewer give to future job seekers? "Be bold," he quotes Edmund Spenser, "be bold, and everywhere be bold."

3

Dealing with Your Needs

If there is one thing you've learned through living with a handicapping condition, whether it is congenital, a result of disease or accident, or a war injury, it is that you will need to hurdle a number of barriers. Although each of us, with or without disabilities, faces barriers, you may at times consider unjust the constant parade of barriers that cross your way. Yet if you are like the thousands upon thousands of persons with disabilities we have come to know personally and through our readings, overcoming obstacles appears to increase your resolve, to add steel to your desire to live the most productive life possible.

"Where there's a will, there's a way." That popular adage is dramatically illustrated in case after case of your persistence to attain your ideal. At the Pacific Missile Test Center at Port Mugo, California, disabled pilots put on an air show. Curtis Brewer, paralyzed from the neck down, is a practicing lawyer and runs his own free legal services organization. A photographer who is legally blind and a victim of multiple sclerosis teaches photography and shows her work in galleries. We have already spoken of our late optometrist who, paralyzed by polio, put himself through optometry school. In his day, there were few laws and minimal technology to aid a person with a handicapping condition.

Today, the situation is considerably altered. Fortunately, attention is now focused on persons with disabilities, and as a result of recent legislation, particularly Sections 503 and 504 of the Rehabilitation Act of 1973, there is increased understanding among the business community and service agencies that hiring persons with disabilities is good business. Thus the barriers, both legal and technical, are slowly eroding. However, we are only on the threshold. Much still needs to be done. Creative problem solvers engaged in producing new technologies for easier travel and better adaptations in the workplace need to be encouraged to continue their activities through the support of business and government. Yet although there are, as Robert Frost said, "miles to go," the current state of the art indicates that inroads are slowly but surely being made to assure you a place in the mainstream.

In this chapter we shall explore some of the methods now available for coping with the working world. We cannot hope to cover the remarkable number of inventions and designs that persons with handicapping conditions have developed for their own use. These adaptations are as unique and widespread as the inventions of the human mind and prove that in the last analysis, it may be your own ingenuity that will be the major force in the solution of your problems.

Who are you? According to Section 504 regulations, you may have:

1.   A physical or mental impairment that substantially limits one or more major life activities, such as caring for yourself, performing manual tasks, walking, seeing, hearing, speaking, breathing, learning and working.

2.   A record of such an impairment, history of, or misclassification as having a mental or physical impairment that substantially limits one or more major life activities. Included are illnesses such as emotional, mental, heart disease or cancer that have been overcome. Under Section 504 you are protected from discrimination on the basis of these past conditions.

3.   You have been regarded as having an impairment. This definition includes: (a) a physical or mental impairment

that does not limit major life activities but is treated by the institution as if such limitation exists; (b) a physical or mental impairment that does limit major life activities only as a result of the attitudes of others toward your impairment; (c) neither a physical or mental impairment, but treated as having one. These conditions may include persons who have a limp, a disfiguring scar, dwarfism, etc.

The thrust of the law is to ensure that such diseases and conditions as orthopedic, visual, speech and hearing impairments, cerebral palsy, epilepsy, muscular dystrophy, multiple sclerosis, cancer, heart disease, diabetes, mental retardation, emotional illness, specific learning disabilities, perceptual handicaps, brain injury, minimal brain dysfunction, dyslexia and developmental aphasia are guaranteed protection from discrimination under Sections 503 and 504. Included in the list of handicapping conditions are drug addiction and alcoholism with the emphasis, however, that Section 504 applies only to discrimination against qualified persons who are able to perform the essential functions of a job or meet the requisite academic or technical standards despite their handicap. If you have a drug or alcohol addiction, you are protected from discrimination in the marketplace, but are expected to meet the standards of the institution where you work.

Depending upon the nature of your disability and the extent to which you are handicapped by it, the attitude of the non-handicapped world will vary. John Gliedman and William Roth point out, in *The Unexpected Minority,* that nearly all persons with a disability, whether it is obvious or hidden, are seen as incapable of participating in social interactions and assuming responsibilities expected of the nondisabled population. Furthermore, the authors state that the handicapped person is treated with a "specifically medical tolerance, excused from normal role obligations." Society, it appears, misreads the significance of disability, and never treats as entirely human the individual with a disability.

Chipping away at these barriers is perhaps your most formidable task. These attitudes enter into every phase of your life, but particularly appear to cluster around your opportunities to make it in the marketplace. There is no easy solution to breaking down the attitudinal barriers, but perhaps one of the most effective methods is through your employment activities. Your efforts, combined with the efforts of the organizations that serve you, can make entering the mainstream a reality.

Government Resources

Take advantage of your local Office of Vocational Rehabilitation (OVR). This state-federal program is expressly designed to provide vocational rehabilitation to help you become socially and vocationally competent. All persons with emotional, mental or physical disabilities are served through OVR, with the exception of the blind, who are served by the Commission for the Blind and Visually Handicapped. The primary goal of vocational rehabilitation is gainful employment in the most expedient manner.

Essentially the guidelines for OVRs throughout the nation are comparable, but services may vary from state to state. You can expect that you will receive to some degree:

- individual vocational rehabilitation counseling and guidance to help you select and attain a job

- medical examinations, psychological tests, diagnostic vocational evaluations, and other evaluative services to determine the nature and extent of your disability or disabilities, remaining abilities and capacities, need for treatment, possibility for improvement, and vocational potential

- physical restoration, medical, surgical, psychiatric hospital care, and physical, occupational, speech and work therapy to reduce, correct or eliminate your disability

- prosthetic appliances and assistive devices such as artificial limbs, braces, hearing aids, walkers and wheel-chairs, to modify your disability and help you secure your chosen vocational objective

- instruction and training to prepare you for a job
- books and related training materials
- interpreter services for those who are deaf
- maintenance and transportation during restoration and/or training
- equipment, initial stocks, supplies and tools to place you in self-employment
- home and vehicle modification
- business and occupation licenses to help you engage in a selected occupation
- individual placement in a suitable job and follow-up to make sure you are safely and satisfactorily employed

Depending upon your financial circumstances, you may be expected to share the expense of some of the services such as assistive devices and prosthetic appliances; medical, psychiatric, surgical or hospital restoration and services; college or university tuition and fees; licenses, equipment, and tools; and additional costs arising from the rehabilitation program.

Your OVR may also contract services for you such as trade and technical training. Essentially, the purpose of OVR is to see that you become employed as quickly as possible. Emphasis is placed on the least amount of training necessary to get you a job. Placement, therefore, when it doesn't match your goals, may be regarded as a stepping stone toward attainment of long-range plans, particularly if those plans include undergraduate or graduate education.

Take advantage also of other vocational and rehabilitative services available to you. Your state employment service counselor will be able to assist you in finding a service that is geared to your particular needs. Many of the private, nonprofit agencies are equipped to handle vocational counseling, assist you or provide for rehabilitation that will involve the use of the most advanced technological equipment, and to provide access to jobs through their job development programs (see chapter 6, "Job Sources").

Reasonable Accommodation

Perhaps the problem most ubiquitous and resistant to solution is the barrier of accessibility. According to the Urban Institute, obstacles to access can affect as many as 23.3 million adults between the ages of 18 and 64. In addition, some 2 million disabled persons are institutionalized and could become productive if this stumbling block was removed. The U.S. Office of Education estimates that some 8 million youths, aged 3 to 21, are disabled enough to require special education in public schools. And a quarter of our senior citizens aged 65 and over are disabled. These figures add up to a staggering 35 to 50 million disabled Americans who are handicapped by their environment.

Accessibility to buildings is not a recurring expense, nor does it add greatly to the expense of construction. New public buildings must now be accessible to all persons by law. Some states have passed laws requiring that all new buildings be accessible. Older buildings or services may be adapted at minimal expense with proper planning. There are a number of architectural organizations specifically geared to assist industry, colleges, universities and transportation facilities to update their facilities. The term "reasonable accommodation" applies to what organizations and institutions are expected to do to make their facilities accessible to you. To encourage accessibility, the federal government has funds available through state and local governments from general revenue sharing and community development block grants to local public works money. The U.S. Office on Handicapped Individuals (OHI) and the Architectural and

Transportation Barriers Compliance Board (A&TBCB) have compiled a resource guide called *Architectural Barriers Removal.* Another useful guide is the *Resource Guide to Literature on Barrier-Free Environments.* These guides are available from the Architectural and Transportation Barriers Compliance Board, Washington, D.C. 20201. Suggestions that you may be able to make to business companies about tax credits and sources of funding for removal of architectural barriers can at times lead to job attainment.

An organization or institution is expected to make its premises accessible to you. Accessibility includes ramps, widened doorways and redesign of restroom facilities, and may also include job restructuring, part-time or modified work schedules, acquisition or modification of equipment or devices, the provision of readers or interpreters and other similar actions. Interpretations of the law suggest that employers keep an open mind when they think of reasonable accommodation, since handicapped employees may use uncommon techniques for performing job functions. The word *reasonable* is pivotal here, for employers are required to hire you when the accommodation will not cause undue hardship. Thus, your qualifications for a job and the employer's interpretation of the accommodations for your handling that job may be subject to different interpretations.

Along the same lines, if, following a medical examination, your condition is deemed to be a threat to your safety or the safety of others on the job, the employer need not hire you. Such a problem might arise if you have impaired manual skills and apply for a job requiring manual dexterity in a laboratory where hazardous materials are handled. Obviously, the employer would be justified in discrimination on the grounds that the job might be injurious to your or your colleagues' health.

The employer, then, must make reasonable accommodation provided that the accommodation does not cause undue hardship. Undue hardship is considered in relation to the nature and cost of the accommodation needed; the effect of this cost on the organization with respect to the number of employees, number and type of facilities and size of budget; and the type of operation, including the composition and structure of the work force.

Furthermore, accommodations should be determined only on a case-by-case basis. Since an accommodation is highly individualized, what is appropriate for you may not be suitable for another person with a similar disability. Before accommodations are made, it is advisable to discuss the nature and need of your disability with your future employer in order to make suggestions for modification. Consider the following questions when you meet with an employer.

1. Is an accommodation necessary for performance of my duties?

2. What effect will the accommodation have on the company's operation and on other employees' performance?

3. To what extent does the accommodation compensate for my limitations?

4. Will the accommodation give me the opportunity to function, participate, or compete on a more equal basis with coworkers?

5. Will the accommodation benefit others (both handicapped and nonhandicapped individuals)?

6. Are there alternatives that will accomplish the same purpose?

Specific Modifications of the Worksite

Bearing these questions in mind, some of the specific modifications you can expect in the worksite include the rearrangement of files or shelves for accessibility if you are in a wheelchair; the widening of areas between fixtures to allow room for your wheelchair; the placement of braille labels or tactile cues on shelves to enable you who are visually impaired to identify the contents; the raising or lowering of equipment controls to hand or foot operation to accommodate your needs if you are physically impaired; the installation of touch-tone telephones if you cannot dial; the installation of special holding devices on desks, machines and benches; the provision of a speaker phone, an extension arm or gooseneck to hold a phone receiver; the provision of special heating or air-conditioning units; the use of a tape recorder, dictaphone, voice writer for taking dictation; the installation of a light sensor probe enabling you who are visually handicapped to operate a switchboard; the installation of a signalman that causes a lamp to flash on and off when the phone rings; and the installation of a light connected to a bell to signal you when there is a fire drill, lunch break or closing time.

Admittedly, these modifications just scratch the surface of the many and varied methods by which an employer can adjust the worksite. They have been chosen to illustrate that accommodations in the workplace need not be extensive, expensive or complicated. This is an important message to bring to your future employer.

Modifications of Written Examinations

Certain changes in the test administration such as extra time, small group or individual testing can be considered a valid modification. You might also need to have questions read to you, or to have someone write down your answers, or if the test instructions are given verbally and you are hearing-handicapped, to have these instructions written or interpreted in sign language. Some parts of the test content may be inappropriate for you. You may need to demonstrate your skill at the actual task rather than take a formal paper and pencil test. If you feel, when taking an examination for a job, that certain modifications can help you to do better on the test, discuss them with the test administrator. If he or she cannot make the adjustments, discuss the situation with your vocational counselor, who will, in all likelihood, be able to suggest alternatives to accommodate your needs.

Work Schedule Adjustment

You may find that the average forty-hour-week, nine-to-five routine and rush-hour negotiation is beyond your physical capacity.

It is highly likely that you can arrange with an employer to adjust your schedule. Perhaps you can begin work earlier and leave earlier to avoid the rush hour. Or you may need a flexible schedule to accommodate weekly medical treatment. If you are diabetic, you will need to work a regular schedule, even though others holding comparable jobs are required to work differing shifts. Part-time or a combination of part-time and home work may be most suitable for you. Many persons with handicapping conditions have been able to work out equitable scheduling adjustments that meet both their own and their employers' needs. It is important that you do not take advantage of your disability. If you can work the same hours and shifts as other workers, by all means do so, but if you need accommodation, find equitable ways for working out the kinks with your employer.

If you are a federal employee, you might investigate the Federal Employee's Part-Time Career Employment Act of 1978. This alternative experimental work scheduling program encourages various accommodations such as flexible working hours, extended rest periods and the use of home as an official work location.

A note of caution. Only those companies doing business of $2500 or more with the federal government must comply with the regulations of Sections 503 and 504. Institutions that receive federal assistance must also comply. If a company or institution does not do business with the federal government or receive assistance in some manner, that organization is not covered by the law.

The Transportation Barrier

Providing adequate and accessible transportation makes a good deal of sense in a budget-minded economy. The Urban Institute estimates that at least $1.3 billion could be saved annually if more public transportation were accessible to disabled Americans to get to and from jobs. This would be reflected in the $40 billion spent annually by federal programs now serving disabled citizens, most of which goes for income maintenance. The irony of these statistics is that if persons who are disabled are allowed to work at full potential, those programs serving their needs would diminish, while at the same time the contributions of the disabled to society in terms of tax dollars would grow.

Certainly one of the most pressing problems when considering a job is mobility. Notwithstanding the Section 504 mandate for access to all public services, the transportation systems of large cities present staggering normal transport problems, quite apart from the problem of modification for the handicapped. This situation wasn't helped by former transportation chief Drew Lewis when he rescinded rules requiring recipients of federal mass transit funds to build wheelchair lifts into all new buses and install elevators into existing rapid rail systems. Mr. Lewis called the ruling an "inordinate inflexible burden on local communities," and stated that the new rulings would allow communities to best decide for themselves how to meet the transportation needs of disabled people. At present writing, the interim rule that will be replaced by permanent rule after public hearings allows transit authorities to certify to the department that appropriate efforts are being made to provide service to handicapped riders. These services can take a variety of forms at the discretion of the community. That does not mean that all transportation services will be abolished. Taxi vouchers may be provided, some buses may be made accessible, other accommodations provided.

The situation is unfortunate. At present, disabled citizens who must rely on such paratransit as cabs (which may or may not be vouchered) cannot claim the expense as a tax deduction, even though their taxes help subsidize the very public transportation system they cannot use. With new systems such as San Francisco's BART, accessibility is built into the design, but in the old systems, as heretofore stated, there are problems that create immeasurable human and financial cost to the individual and society.

Answers do exist. What is needed is the cooperation of both government and business to form an alliance to produce the best equipment and services available. Some of the highly marketable ideas include:

Van Adaptation

Curtis Brewer, paralyzed from the neck down, had a van adapted that accommodated his wheelchair and also served as a traveling office.

Car Adaptation

Currently on the market.

Electric Cars

Paul Bates, a polio victim, quadraplegic, with only a slight movement of his head and movement in three fingers, designed—with the help of Reg Maling of POSSUM (manufacturers of equipment for the severely disabled)—an electric car (or float, as it is called in England) to give him mobility to carry on his job as a salesman.

Taxicab Adaptation

Perhaps one of the brightest ideas on the horizon is the adaptation of the Checker Cab or a car of that size by Joe Parriott of the Margaret Gate Institute in New York City. Parriott and his colleagues have developed an inexpensive method for adapting the car to accommodate one or two wheelchairs. The cost of transportation would be at the same rates as other taxi services, but would afford the rider the dignity of traveling to and from work in a nonconspicuous accommodation. An added feature of this adaptation is that it can also accommodate a baby carriage, complete with baby.

Wheelchair News

The wheelchair itself is undergoing a rejuvenation. Engineers have been examining wheelchairs for some time and find that although they are functional, they are grossly inefficient. Professor Roger Glaser at the Wright State University in Dayton found that wheelchair travel is only 5 percent efficient; 95 percent of the work put into making the chair move is wasted in the form of heat. Apparently, the arm muscles are not equipped for locomotion, especially the kind of locomotion requiring synchronized action of the arms. Another energy drain is the motion of the backward swing of the arms, and more energy is expended on the force needed to hang on and turn the hand rims.

According to Glaser, one solution for designing a more energy-efficient wheelchair is attaching a contraption that looks like a unicycle turned upside down. It clamps onto a standard wheelchair and allows you to drive it by pedaling with your hands in an alternating method. The pedals also steer the chair. Five gears match the ease of pedaling to your strength, the surface and incline on which you're traveling. The attachment costs $500 and is available at many orthopedic supply stores. It does have the disadvantage of being cumbersome. Nevertheless, Glaser feels that the technology for a more compact model is available, but pressure must be brought to bear upon the manufacturers for its development.

Computers have made motorized wheelchairs smart. One of the designs engineered at Stanford University in Palo Alto moves the wheelchair in the direction of a head turn. Ultrasound distance sensors feed information into a microcomputer. A tilt of your head establishes the direction in which the wheelchair moves. Other sensors detect obstacles. The designers hope that this system can be added to the standard motorized chair for as little as $500.

A chair, designed primarily for indoor use, will spin on its axis, allowing movement in all directions, including sideways. This flexibility is made possible through the use of three wheels, constructed of eight rollers to the wheel. Maneuverability is also a feature of the omnidirectional ambulatory chair, designed by Carl Mason and currently in experiment with V.A. engineers in New York City. This chair spins on four clusters of small wheels, is fitted with a seat belt and has a knee brace allowing you to stand up.

It appears possible that in the near future, with the combination of more efficient wheelchairs and a more effective transportation system, hurdling the barrier of getting to and from work will require no more of you than your ability to drive or maneuver your equipment.[1]

Specific Needs and Modifications

For each disability, there appears to be a range of accommodations, depending upon function. Some of you may need a complex set of modifications to perform your work most effectively, while others may need only minimal adjustments. However, whatever your disability, it is wise to contact the association or service connected with that disability to determine the most recent technological developments. (See Appendix III for list of organizations.) It might be expedient, however, to examine briefly some of the modifications and adaptations that relate to specific handicapping conditions.

Visually Impaired/Blind

Specific aids for those of you who are blind have a long history. Aggressive medical treatment, to varying degrees can now preserve some sight in a great many cases. Modifications of the workplace for you who are visually impaired may require bright incandescent lighting rather than fluorescent, magnification of materials and larger lettering. Where blindness is present, it is possible to use a wide variety of "reading machines" that scan a printed page and print it instantly in braille, transform letters into tactile symbols on the fingertips, turn letters into tone pat-

---

[1] Adapted from an article by Denise Grady, in *Discover*, September 1981.

terns, spell words out loud, read and reproduce words and sentences in artificial speech and enlarge type and pictures. Tape recorders, In Touch radio, and talking books answer the needs of many of you. Traveling is made accessible through the auspices of a number of rehabilitative organizations. In short, since the invention of braille, aids to help you overcome your disability, both medically and technologically, have grown rapidly. For more information, look at *A Resource Guide: Sensory Aids for Employment of Blind and Visually Impaired Persons,* published by the American Foundation of the Blind.

Deaf/Hearing Impaired

The major problem you face is communicating with the hearing world. If you are not adept at lip reading, conversation with a nonsigning person is tedious both for you and your partner. You probably are equipped with the most sensitive hearing instruments and have amplification equipment such as the teletypewriter acoustic adapter, but it is a good idea also to check with the telephone company and a manufacturer or service organization to be abreast of the latest technological developments.

You are also finding that the hearing world is more aware of you. Films and television programs are either captioned or interpreted in many cases. You can attend large meetings, classes, assemblies and most often find an interpreter on the premises. In the job situation, however, an interpreter may not be present except for the initial period of adjustment. Here, with your employer and colleagues you will need to work out the necessary adaptations for job survival. If problems emerge, contact your vocational counselor.

Epilepsy

There are two million of you in America who have some form of epilepsy. Most of you, 80 percent, are able to work. Your major accommodation lies in taking the proper medication.

Cerebral Palsy

Your condition may need a number of accommodations. Medication has been proven to be effective for control of seizures. Braces, crutches and wheelchairs help you to become mobile. On the job, accommodations of height of equipment, transferring operable levers to accommodate unimpaired limbs, shorter working hours, rest periods are a few of the adjustments that can be easily made. Depending upon your condition you can, together with your counselor and future employer, usually work out a satisfactory routine.

Multiple Sclerosis

The statistics currently available reveal that 82 percent of you who have a mild or moderate form of this disease do work. Modifications of the workplace may include a lesser work load, adequate rest and prompt attention when there are intercurrent infections. However, the range of jobs held by you who are afflicted with the disease covers the entire gamut of occupations, bearing witness to the fact that whatever job you aspire to, accommodation is possible.

Muscular Dystrophy

For many of you with this disease, no adaptation is necessary. Eventually, you may need to use a wheelchair, and depending upon the progression of the disease, still continue to work effectively.

Cystic Fibrosis

There is no reason why you can't work in the majority of jobs for which you will interview. Difficulties may arise if the job involves heavy physical labor or is excessively sedentary. Exposure to dust, fumes and extremes of temperatures is also counterproductive. Depending upon the severity of your condition, your may find that a temporary (one woman found becoming a substitute teacher ideal) or part-time job or a shortened day will provide all you need in the form of modification.

Quadraplegic/Paraplegic

We have described a number of devices "in the works" on redesigning the wheelchair. On the market are powered wheelchairs that allow you to control movement even though you are nearly totally paralyzed or grossly spastic. These machines are equipped with emergency functions—flasher, horn, headlight and siren; automatic alarms—tip-over siren; select speed range, lapboard mounted cassette recorder to take notes and do dictation; making and answering telephone calls by remote control, remote control of TV, radio and household appliances; the operation of a communication device; typing or using a computer. Companies making such products for the severely impaired include Possum, Inc. and Prentke Romich Company. And on the horizon is the use of Capuchin monkeys to act as miniature servants.

Spina Bifida

With your braces, crutches or wheelchair, there is no reason that you cannot find work.

Stroke and Hemiplegia

Vocational rehabilitation centers have been successful in helping persons like yourself to relearn lost skills and abilities. You may even be able to return to the job you previously held.

Kidney Disease

With the 1973 legislation providing federal payment for kidney transplants and dialysis, there is no reason why you cannot compete in the marketplace, provided you are within reach of a dialysis treatment center.

Cancer

Cancer is not contagious. There is no reason why you cannot work or continue to work. If you suspect discrimination, contact the State Office of the Handicapped or your mayor's Office of the Handicapped.

Diabetes

Basically you are able to work at the same kinds of jobs and at the same levels as your co-workers, provided that you are on a regular schedule. A pressure job where you skip lunches or dinners is not advisable. Manual labor should pose little problem since exercise is good for you. However, it is best to avoid hazardous work, especially if you are insulin-dependent.

Mentally Restored

Your accommodation on a job is for the most part intrinsic rather than extrinsic. You probably know the kind of work situation that "bugs" you, the kind of pressure to avoid, the relationships you need to form on the job, the amount of information you want to reveal to your fellow employees about yourself. If your breakdown was induced by untenable work situations, then you need to find a different kind of work. If you have not conquered unreasonable fears such as using elevators, traveling where there are large crowds of people, crossing streets, using electrical equipment, you are best off seeking employment where you will deal minimally with these situations. Use the support of your counseling services when returning to work. They are geared to help you make the needed adjustment.

Learning Disabilities

Chances are you have been using technological devices such as tape recorders, cassettes, calculators, books on tape or typewriters throughout your academic career. Most of these aids are standard office equipment and your preferred use of them should present little or no problem. Your choice of job will no doubt be governed by the skills you have acquired and your own methods of adaptation.

Slow Learners

You know that you can work in any number of jobs. Your only problem is that you learn more slowly than most people. But when you learn a task you learn it well. Your main hurdle is to persuade an employer that you can do the job. Often you will have to demonstrate a skill, rather than talk about it. We have heard about so-called mentally retarded persons who have invented simple designs of equipment to improve on performance accuracy. Remember, the most important thing for you is to show the employer what you can do.

The message generated from these capsule descriptions is that it should be possible for you to find work provided you have the proper accommodations. The federal government, organizations such as the Veterans Administration and those organizations involved in specific handicapping conditions are working toward that goal. In addition, funding is being generated for development of new technology. A program now under way, sponsored by grants from the National Science Foundation and the Radio Shack Division of the Tandy Corporation, is seeking new methods for modification. The search features a nationwide competition to encourage ideas for applying computer technology to solve difficulties faced by you in learning, working and successfully adapting to home and community settings.

PART II

THE JOB HUNT

4

KNOW THE LAW AND USE IT

With the advent of National Employ the Handicapped Week, instituted in 1977, the employment needs of handicapped persons were sharply brought into focus. Status was conferred on this event through a proclamation by the President's Committee on Employment of the Handicapped, stating:

. . . Whereas it is incumbent on all citizens to recognize the ability of handicapped people to contribute to their own lives and the greater society of which they are a part, and whereas employment at the highest level for which one is qualified is a right not to be abridged by reason of physical or mental handicap, and whereas physical, environmental and attitudinal barriers prevent handicapped people from full participation in the world of work.

Now, therefore, be it resolved, that the citizens of this (city, state, country) celebrate the National Employ the Handicapped Week with their increased efforts to eliminate those barriers, to the end that all handicapped individuals have access to maximally satisfying and productive employment.

These sentiments are the fortunate outgrowth of the Rehabilitation Act of 1973, Sections 501, 502, 503, 504, that specifically address the area of equal access to job opportunities for the disabled.

Affirmative Action

Section 501 of the Rehabilitation Act expressly deals with government agencies. Each agency must have an affirmative action plan that spells out how the agency proposes to hire and advance persons with handicapping conditions. The federal government has been explicit in seeking compliance from its agencies and has published a number of pamphlets stating clear and positive direction for implementation.

Affirmative action also reaches into the private sector under the regulations of Sections 502 and 503. This law affects approximately three million businesses in the United States. Any company that is under contract with the federal government for more than $2,500 must take affirmative action to hire individuals with handicapping conditions.

Larger companies doing business with the government for $50,000 or more and having at least fifty employees are required to develop an affirmative action program that includes an affirmative action clause in each of its contracts or subcontracts. This clause must include the following statements:

1.   The contractor agrees not to discriminate against a qualified handicapped person, but will hire, advance and treat such person without discrimination.

2.   The contractor shall abide by all Department of Labor rules and regulations.

3.   The contractor will post notices of affirmative action in conspicuous places around the plant and office.

4.   The contractor will include the affirmative action clause in all subcontracts or purchase orders of more than $2,500.

5.   When there is no compliance, the contractor will be declared in default.

It is evident that employment of the handicapped extends beyond the hiring process. Job assignments, promotions, transfers, upward training, working conditions, pension rights and the like must be accessible to every employee. Veterans, both disabled and nondisabled, can also take advantage of affirmative action through the Vietnam Era Veterans Readjustment Assistance Act. Employers who have federal contracts of $10,000 or more must comply with affirmative action policy.

Discrimination and Accessibility

Discrimination against the handicapped in every organization and institution in the United States receiving federal money is further determined through the regulations of Section 504. Every institution in the United States that receives federal assistance must take steps to assure that there is no discrimination against persons who have disabilities. Since the majority of institutions receive some kind of federal assistance, they are required to provide fair treatment for persons applying for employment in schools, colleges, hospitals, nursing homes, social service agencies and other nonprofit organizations.

Section 502 has strengthened the Architectural Barriers Act of 1968 (Public Law 90-480) that decreed all buildings constructed, leased or altered with federal funds since the passage of the act be accessible to the handicapped. Through a series of amendments to this law, design standards for the construction and alteration of buildings and facilities owned or leased by the government have been developed. Essentially what Section 502 adds to the Architectural Barriers Act is a requirement that every institution in the United States receiving federal assistance take steps to assure that there is no discrimination by reason of environment against handicapped persons.

In essence, it is up to the employer, whether it is a business, educational or nonprofit organization, to examine the physical or mental requirements of a job and determine if persons screened from the opportunity of applying for that job are denied that opportunity based on accessibility. If accessibility is found to be lacking, the job requirements need to be eliminated or modified unless it can be proven that they are job-related and consistent with business needs and safe performance.

Reasonable accommodation must be made unless the employer can show it would create undue hardship on the business. Accommodation need not be extensive. It might involve inexpensive procedures such as putting a light over a deaf worker's bench that will flash whenever a bell is rung, amplifying telephones, breaking work into small units for slow and retarded workers. For more information on reasonable accommodation, see chapter 3.

Reaching Out

The employer is also required to recruit for persons with disabilities. Listing of job vacancies with state employment agencies and state vocational rehabilitation offices, private employment agencies, organizations of and for handicapped persons and with schools for handicapped students is a method by which employers can make known the fact that vacancies exist. These outreach efforts are especially important to you, since they provide the opportunity for tapping a number of different job sources.

Recognizing that removal of barriers might cause considerable financial hardship, Congress passed the Tax Reform Act of 1976. This act grants businesses taxable deductions for removal of architectural and transportation barriers. The maximum deduction is $25,000 per taxpayer for any taxable year. This incentive makes it possible for businesses to meet the guidelines for constructing or reconstructing facilities to make their premises accessible to the disabled.

Another tax advantage may be gained through hiring handicapped persons. Employers who hire full-time qualified handicapped individuals may receive up to $3,000 in tax credit for wages paid that employee for the first year of employment, and up to $1,500 for wages paid that employee for the second year. Employees who are hired through this arrangement must be referred and/or certified by a state vocational rehabilitation agency. Other employees who can also participate include disabled workers who have been receiving SSI benefits, and can submit proof of same.

Your Safeguards

The law has a built-in system of safeguards to ensure that your rights to a job and promotion are not abused. However, you will need to identify yourself as handicapped to take advantage of these rights. It is your choice to give or to withhold this information. If you choose to give this information voluntarily, it will be kept strictly confidential except in the case of the supervisor or manager who will need it to make suitable working accommodations and investigate work restrictions, and the first-aid staff who will need to be informed regarding possible emergency treatment. However, if you choose not to divulge this information, you will not be subject to disciplinary treatment.

Your employer must post a notice advising the employees that the affirmative action program is in effect. This notice should contain the following information:

> . . . if you have a handicap and would like to be considered under the affirmative action program, please let us know. This information is voluntary and will be kept strictly confidential except in the case of:
>
> (1)   the supervisor or manager who will need the information to make suitable working accommodations and investigate work restrictions;
>
> (2)   the first-aid staff who will be informed regarding possible emergency treatment.

Do you get the same wages? Yes, for the most part. Federal wage and hour standards apply generally to employees engaged in interstate or foreign commerce, or in the production of goods, or in any activity that is covered by the standards. If you are working for contractors performing on most federally financed or assisted construction projects, or providing services under contract to federal agencies, there are special standards. These standards require that you receive no less than the wages and fringe benefits prevailing in the locality as determined by the Secretary of Labor, and that daily and weekly overtime compensation be paid.

The Department of Labor has set minimum wage standards to be progressively increased over a four-year period until the Federal Minimum Wage is reached for the blind and other severely handicapped who work in sheltered workshops. Begun in the fall of 1980, and on an anniversary date thereafter, current employees must be paid a minimum of 70 percent of the federal minimum wage rather than the rate of 50 percent. In the second year, the rate rises to 80 percent, 90 percent in the third, and 100 percent in the fourth year. Workers entering the workshop program will start at 50 percent and then on each anniversary date follow the increase procedures.

Therefore, you are protected by the same minimum wage and hour standards of any worker, unless you are in a special certified program such as a sheltered workshop.

Rights Abused? File a Complaint!

You have a right to complain if a federal contractor or subcontractor refuses to let you file an application but accepts others; you are fired or laid off and others are not affected; you are passed over for promotion for which you are qualified; you are paid less than others for comparable work; you are placed in a segregated seniority line; you are placed in a segregated workplace; you are left out of training or an apprenticeship program; or you believe that the reason for any of these acts is a result of your disability, the history of your disability, or your being regarded as disabled.

If you suspect you are not receiving fair treatment, file a complaint, but be prepared to wait for a hearing. As with so many federal agencies, the wheels of justice move slowly. At present writing there is a serious backlog of cases. These following agencies may be able to assist you:

- Disability Rights Center, 1346 Connecticut Avenue N.W., Suite 1124, Washington, D.C. 20036.
- Mainstream, Inc., 1200 Fifth Street N.W., Washington, D.C. 20005 (212-424-8089).
- Affirmative Action, Office of Federal Contract Compliance, Department of Labor, Washington, D.C. 20210.

The State of the Art

How these laws are interpreted and implemented varies with each organization and/or municipality. The concern, of course, is funding. Since the inception of the Law, budget managers have complained that Section 504 creates undue hardship on city governments where large expenditures for making all municipally owned buildings accessible to persons with handicapping conditions would create tremendous financial liability. These matters appear to be worsening, especially in cities where facilities were constructed many years ago.

On the other hand, large corporations such as DuPont, Sears Roebuck, Con Edison and IBM proudly highlight their record of hiring and promoting persons with handicapping conditions. The nature and extent of jobs filled by workers with handicapping conditions in these organizations range from mailroom clerk to executive.

Nevertheless, full participation by all organizations, both in the public and private sectors, still remains an unfulfilled dream. Figures from the 1970 census (1980 figures have not been published as of this writing) indicate that only 42 percent of you are employed. This number may since have risen due to the Rehabilitation Act of 1973, especially since several important factors are now working in your favor.

1. According to Bowe in *Rehabilitating America* the cost of maintaining handicapped people in dependency roles has increased each year, i.e., $114 billion in 1970, expected to rise to $210 billion in the 1980s.

2. Employers are demonstrating their willingness to comply with the legislation and hire qualified candidates. Tax incentives and tax credits make hiring the handicapped good business.

3. You are becoming actively involved through your advocacy groups and your own personal commitment to making the law work for you.

You are by no means alone. In 1981, the International Year of Disabled Persons, the United Nations focused on your rights, declaring that:

Disabled persons have the right to economic and social security and to a decent living. They have the right according to their capabilities to secure and retain employment or to engage in a useful, productive and remunerative occupation and to join trade unions.

Advocacy Is the Name of the Game

Although the federal laws assuring you of your right to a job are powerful and all-encompassing, it is the human factor that provides the gas on which the legal motor turns. Through your efforts the employment picture can brighten. It is estimated that from 10 to 15 percent of the people in a community have a significant physical, mental or learning disability. By joining with or, if no organization exists, developing a community action group, you can assure that your needs and the needs of other disabled persons in your community are being addressed.

Look at it this way. Some 30 to 35 million Americans are disabled to some degree. In the working force alone, among the 121 million Americans between the ages of 16 and 65, over 11.2 million are disabled. Translated into percentages, that figure means that some 9 percent of the working population is disabled, but if given the opportunity and accessibility, this population can become a vital part of the working force.

As we have indicated previously, only some 42 percent of you appear to be working to full potential. And because of this high figure of unemployment, on the whole you do not do as well as the general population. You have less schooling, lower incomes, live in poverty twice as high in proportion to the general population for the very poorest levels, and fewer of you are working.

Is there a better reason for advocacy? Your story needs to be told. Your skills and abilities need to be visible. Your existence as a citizen needs to be reiterated. The public needs to see you, not as a charity case, but as a functioning member of society. Since self-support is one of your prime needs, let's take a chapter from the President's Committee on Employment of the Handicapped, *Mainstreet: Community Action for Disabled Americans—A Guide for Service Organizations.* This booklet, for sale in bulk from the Superintendent of Documents, U.S. Government Printing Office, Washington, D.C., 20402, or in single copy from the President's Committee, is designed to help you form an advocacy group to assure that the rights and needs of disabled citizens are met.

One of the goals is to promote job opportunities. Although there are a number of organizations involved in this project, some of which overlap in function, others which duplicate functions and others which work in tandem with each other, there appears to be no matrix of existing organizations, their services and the populations they serve. Your first step might then be, depending upon the size and nature of your community, to organize a council for the purpose of bringing together the existing resources into a comprehensive continuum of services. Your most valuable resource will be your local Committee on Employment of the Handicapped. Some thousand such committees exist in communities throughout the United States. If one does not exist where you live, you might consider starting one. A second resource is any veterans' group in your community. Disabled veterans make up a large portion of the disabled population. Primarily your goals for this council should be:

- to develop a climate of acceptance of handicapped individuals

- to bring together agencies and organizations into a forceful coalition that can target the problem and deal with the problems impeding full opportunity for the disabled

- to provide for a common meeting ground between government agencies and elected officials, business unions and other parties and yourselves to discuss issues and concerns

Getting a Committee Started

You will need some influential members to get your committee started. Meet with the mayor and solicit his or her support. This support may be offered in terms of a representative to the committee, meeting space, clerical support and some financing. Representatives should be drawn from the State Employment Office, Chamber of Commerce, vocational rehabilitation centers, Veterans Administration, secondary and postsecondary educational institutions, civic groups, unions, churches, synagogues, community organizations, other veterans groups, other handicapped groups, major business corporations, employers and other persons or organizations that you see as influential in your community.

If you have difficulty in obtaining the cooperation of City Hall, ask the Governor's Committee on the Handicapped for aid and resource.

All this groundwork will take time. Expect to spend from three to four months gathering information, identifying needs, meeting with other community groups and contacting the mayor's office and/or governor's committee. If you have at least ten members in your nuclear group, the leg (arm, ear, eye) work can be considerably shortened.

Committee Action

Your campaign can be geared to a multilevel approach encompassing direct contact with business firms and organizations in your community, publicity and public relations, the preparation of a guide, mounting a job fair, and running seminars for industry leaders. Or you may choose to concentrate on only one aspect of the campaign. Your choice of activity will be governed by the number of members on your committee, your budget and your time commitment. However, whether you concentrate on one aspect or plan a comprehensive campaign, you will want to follow these simple guidelines.

Employer Visit

This visit should involve a presentation to the business manager or personnel director about the advantages of employing the handicapped. The presentation is founded on the premise that people with handicapping conditions are dependable employees who should not be treated differently from other employees except in terms of accessibility and adaptation when necessary. Be ready to share information about the benefits of an affirmative action program. Offer your assistance as an organization in helping to solve problems with hiring, placement and advancement. Lastly, leave a brochure or newsletter with the prospective employer, thus affording him or her the opportunity of reading more about your services. If you have not developed any literature, write to the President's Committee for quantities of the pocket guide, *Affirmative Action for Disabled People*.

Publicity/Public Relations

This subcommittee should be charged with developing flyers, brochures and posters advocating jobs for the disabled. Recently, IBM ran a full-page ad in the *New York Times* describing one of its employees, Richard Coleman, a disabled Vietnam veteran. Coleman began selling computers for IBM, moved rapidly up the ladder to teaching customers how to get the most out of their computers. Clearly, IBM's message is that employees with disabilities are as capable, reliable and ambitious and just as likely to succeed as nondisabled workers. Publicity of this kind serves two purposes—i.e., good public relations for the company and the fostering of public awareness that a worker with a handicapping condition is capable of performing a job.

Case histories make interesting and uplifting reading. You might want to survey your community in order to compile a list of those persons who have overcome the odds to "make it" in business, industry and their private lives.

A good deal of your public relations effort will be geared toward the fostering of acceptance, changing attitudes about persons with disabilities. A number of organizations have made attitude change one of their primary goals. The Association for the Help of Retarded Adults for one has exerted great efforts to bring about awareness of the fact that retarded adults can do many jobs as effectively as persons within the normal IQ range. The vocational rehabilitation agencies are also involved in changing attitudes, as are the mayor's and governor's committees. You will want to draw on all these resources when you plan your own goals and objectives.

The outgrowth of your public relations campaign might be the establishment of yearly awards to companies and individuals who are genuinely interested and concerned about furthering employment for the handicapped. Prepare a *certificate of recognition* or *appreciation* that can be presented as an annual event. It is often possible to involve your local and state government in developing these award presentations. You might also want to look into the national recognition award presented by the President's Committee on Employment of the Handicapped. Each year two employers are chosen for outstanding achievement in hiring handicapped employees. One award is for companies with less than two hundred employees, the other for those with more than two hundred employees.

Prepare a Guide

The work of this subcommittee is extensive, time-consuming and extremely worthwhile. A guide to services in your community will be used by the business community, other organizations and disabled individuals. You will probably find that collecting and collating all the information about resources in your community will open doors to a great many new job possibilities. Preparation of this guide will take from four to six months, depending upon the number of individuals who work on it. When the machinery is in motion, however, you will find that the work progresses rapidly.

Depending upon the needs of your community, your guide can contain both access to services for the handicapped and the names of firms and organizations prepared to offer assistance on architectural problems, adaptation of equipment and problem solving.

A quick way to assemble information is to prepare a form for respondents. In this way, all the information gathered is uniform in style and can be submitted easily to a printer.

Unions

A valuable resource to your organization is union involvement. If it is not possible to establish a separate subcommittee, assign one individual to develop union representation. The cooperation of unions in placing and protecting the rights of disabled workers is a goal that needs to be developed. One of your objectives should be to determine what individual unions are doing to promote the same protection to disabled workers that is conferred upon the nondisabled. In industries where disability may result from the hazards of the job, the union efforts in this regard are an issue of major importance.

Run a Job Fair

The job fair provides an opportunity for both employer and potential employee to look each other over without the formal trappings of the interview. It is a means for bringing together the business community, educational resources, rehabilitative resources and other interested groups into one area where both disabled and nondisabled persons are encouraged to explore similarities and differences.

A job fair can be run in cooperation with your local high school, junior college, trade or vocational school, or college. You will probably want to invite the various counseling services in your community such as the Veterans Administration, Office of Vocational Rehabilitation, State Employment Office, if these organizations are not already a part of your committee. Many private organizations such as the Association for the Help of Retarded Citizens, Jewish Vocational Services, associations for the blind and deaf, crippled children and adults (see Appendix III for complete listing) have their own referral services and should be included in this enterprise if a chapter exists in your vicinity.

By all means make invitation to the business community a priority. Business will see the job fair as a means of good public relations. Although jobs may not exist in a business at the time of the fair, the swiftness with which the ebbs and tides of the economy turn can alter a company's need for manpower overnight. Alert managers are always on the lookout for talented employees.

To run a job fair, you will need a large space. Try for a school auditorium, civic center, meeting room, armory, or the like. Try to get the space donated. If you cannot get free space, you will have to charge for exhibit space. For example, if you rent 800 square feet, costing $400, the rental space can be divided into 8' by 10' spaces at $40.00 each.

You will also need to develop a brochure describing the event. Send it to companies, agencies, programs, educational institutions, organizations for disabled people and community groups. Start a publicity campaign. Get coverage on radio, TV and in your local newspapers. Develop a poster barrage. Place posters in every conceivable place where people shop or go for entertainment.

You'll have to organize transportation pools for disabled who cannot get to the fair any other way. This pool must be organized in advance so that disabled people wanting to be at the fair will be sure to reach the premises.

Then make a floor plan of the exhibition area. Develop a program of the day's events. Draw up plans for a seminar. This seminar can be part of the job fair or a separate activity. The main purpose of a seminar is to help managers understand the needs of disabled workers. The Institute for the Crippled and Disabled in New York City has, as part of its rehabilitation program, a series of seminars to help managers solve problems in using disabled workers effectively. These seminars combine problem-solving approaches with awareness factors. In New York City, members from over forty large companies and organizations have attended the seminar, and although one or two days of intensive workshop experience hardly produces answers to all questions, participants do feel that they are helped by the practical approach. Your seminar should plan to cover the following topics:

> awareness of handicapping conditions
>
> dos and don'ts for dealing with persons who have a variety of handicapping conditions
>
> simulation exercises

explorations of hidden attitudes

discipline of a disabled worker

punctuality

reasonable accommodation

problem solving

Financing the Project

A great deal of the spade work can be accomplished through the service of volunteers. However, it is possible also to tap into federal funding. One of the drawbacks to federal funding, however, is the time lapse between proposal writing and funding. Also, when money is tight, chances that your proposal will be funded are slim. Nevertheless, it is a good idea to make the attempt. You can find out about sources from Publication No. E 180-2201, *Federal Assistance for Programs Servicing the Handicapped,* U.S. Department of Education, Office for Handicapped Individuals, Washington, D.C. 20202.

You should also investigate the possibility of soliciting full or partial funding from a large business or business association. The mayor's committee or the governor's committee may also have some funds available for various aspects of your endeavors. Finances are often a result of the composition of your committee, its commitment and its access to resources in the community. Key members of your committee may be instrumental in obtaining the supportive help necessary to keep your council financially solvent.

A last word: Be sure to write to the President's Committee on Employment of the Handicapped, Washington, D.C. 20210, for a complete listing of their publications, brochures and catalogues.

GREGORY MURAKIEWICZ

Born again at St. Vincent's Hospital in 1978—that's how Gregory Murakiewicz describes his successful heart surgery. His steadily weakening and painful condition due to a congenital heart problem threatened to be terminal. But with the help of a mechanical valve, Gregory is now actively engaged in both work and play.

After his operation, Gregory attended graduate school, completed all his credits in a year and received his M.S. in community health education. Still somewhat unsure about his physical ability to withstand the pressures of a daily work schedule, he held back, until his brother alternately commanded him to "go out and find a job," and cajoled him by providing him with a three-piece suit for the purpose.

Being already highly motivated, this incentive was all that Gregory needed. He launched his campaign, setting his sights on working for a government agency, where he felt his background would be most suitable. At the end of seven months, Gregory finally found the job that combined all the aspects for which he had been seeking. As a member of the Office of the State Advocate for the Disabled, he works with persons who have disabilities, helping them locate resources, entitlements and benefits. He is also involved in an outreach program that brings messages of help and assistance into the community.

Gregory's activist interests extend beyond the workplace. In his spare time, he is chairperson of a local citizens' health action coalition. When asked how he finds time in his busy schedule to devote to this project, he replied: "Health is a very important issue to me, personally, professionally and politically." The significance of Gregory's interests, both in his working life and in his volunteer activities is reflected in his response to the question of what does he see himself doing ten years from now. Gregory pauses only for a moment—"Why, more of what I'm doing now, but perhaps on a policy-making or political level."

5

JOB SOURCES

The job market is now more open to you than at any other time in history. Awareness of your capacity as an independent citizen brought about both by the affirmative action laws and by the grassroots activity of you and organizations to which you belong has created if not a landslide, at least a trickle of acceptance into the world of work. Acceptance is often tied to visibility. In this chapter we will be exploring the many traditional and nontraditional methods for finding work. Interestingly, these methods do not necessarily apply to a person with a disability, but are commonly used by anyone looking for a job. At times, unfortunately, a person with a disability is often too proud or self-conscious to use some of the strategies mentioned here, thus limiting some of the more productive routes. We feel that any self-imposed limitation creates an artificial bind. From our own experience and that of placement counselors in rehabilitative agencies and in public and private organizations, the common thread of advice is that your job search should be thorough and far-reaching. The more sources you investigate, the greater the possibility of opportunities.

Let Them Know

First, you should share your needs with family, relatives and friends. Don't be secretive about the fact that you're ready to work. Enlist their support. Ask as many people as you can if they know of job openings. There is no person currently working or who has worked in the past who has not experienced looking for a job. Some persons have looked for jobs just once or twice during their working careers; others have hopped from job to job annually. But everybody has had the experience at least once of examining the job market and applying for a particular job. Therefore, friends, relatives and acquaintances will not only be able to offer you some excellent advice on job seeking, but also may well be privy to jobs within their organizations where a person with your talents is needed.

Finding Out About Openings

Perhaps the neatest method of getting a job is through the recommendation of a person who knows your capabilities, and who can steer you to the interview before the job is advertised or listed with agencies. We find that organizations tend to give preference to the "personally recommended" job applicant. Reasons for this preference range from confidence in the person doing the recommending to projection that if a good worker recommends an individual then that individual too must be a good worker. This method of getting a job is far more prevalent than one realizes. Often in our follow-up work, we have discovered that although we sent a qualified applicant to the company, the job was subsequently filled by a friend of an employee.

Nevertheless, a "friend at court" is not a guarantee of a job. It does, however, help you to reach that crucial interview stage ahead of other job seekers who are applying through the more formal channels of want ads and agency referrals. The winds of chance constantly buffet opportunities. It is up to you to take advantage, to seize whatever opportunity comes your way. Bear in mind, however, the constant that will follow you in all your job search endeavors; whether you are personally recommended or applying "cold," you will still need those special tools of job communication—resume and subsequent follow-through procedures.

Your Organizations Can Help

In addition to friends, relatives and acquaintances, a second important source of job leads is through the membership of the various organizations with which you are affiliated. These organizations may range from church or synagogue to community to professional associations. Through your volunteer activities with these groups, you will begin to know a number of people who are in a variety of professions and businesses. These people will have an opportunity to observe you in action, get to know you, not only as a personable individual, but as a doer with a proven level of competency.

Volunteer work is finally being accepted as an important indicator of a person's ability. In some colleges, volunteer experience is evaluated for course credit, especially in those programs geared to adult education and alternate routes for getting a college education (see chapter 10). It is also appropriate to include in a resume volunteer experience when that experience is consistent with specific job requirements. In addition, many volunteer jobs are transformed into paid positions when the need is established and funding can be developed. If you have been volunteering in a responsible post, your move into a salaried position holds no threat to the supervisory or managerial staff, since your condition has in no way handicapped you from performing on the job.

Primarily, however, your volunteer work puts you into contact with people you would not ordinarily meet in your everyday routine. You might be rubbing shoulders with executives, administrators, office personnel from a variety of businesses and institutions. The wife of a college dean spends her free time at a large museum. The president of a small manufacturing firm acts as an umpire to the little leaguers in his community. Organizations such as the Rotary Club, Kiwanis, Junior League or Junior Republic all have public service as one of their main objectives. These organizations, to name only a few, are sponsored by members or wives of members of the business community.

Your activities as a volunteer can also lead to jobs with other agencies and community organizations, since many of these organizations form a loose network of services. Lastly, you may have founded your own council (chapter 4) which in itself will be a vital force toward getting the job you want.

Professional Organizations

Professional organizations offer a small but select source of jobs for you. Each profession has at least one association, and in some cases, where there are a great many persons with the same training, as with teachers, more than one association. Some of these associations are formed as unions with dues-paying members; others consist of organizations of individuals who have the same specialized education or training in a particular field. The majority of these organizations and associations hold annual meetings at which time they bring together members who represent local chapters. These meetings may involve educational programs comprised of workshops and seminars, election of new officers, and in many cases a job clinic. Under certain economic conditions the job clinic may be the major activity of the conference.

If the association is large, there will no doubt be local chapters in your state. You may already belong to one or more of these chapters. These chapters often run their own conferences, patterned after the annual conference of the national organization but mounted on a much smaller scale.

A good percentage of these associations will publish a newsletter or journal that can run from a four-page mimeographed flyer to a one hundred-page professionally acclaimed journal. These publications in the majority of cases feature a want ad section. Thus you will have the opportunity of studying the job market nationally for your particular field. Although cost of advertising is often expensive in the journals, you may consider making the investment in order to give yourself nation-wide exposure. The cost of subscribing to the journal is most often included in your membership fee.

There are some professional organizations committed to assisting handicapped individuals. The American Association for the Advancement of Science for one has developed a three-level program. It includes major efforts in technical assistance to disabled individuals, their parents, teachers, employers and others in the areas pertaining to science education and careers as well as the employment of handicapped individuals in the science professions; their third and newest project is the improvement of locomotion, sensory and manipulatory capability through low-cost technological aids. For more information, write to Project on the Handicapped in Science, Office of Opportunities in Science, American Association for Advancement of Science, 1766 Massachusetts Ave., N.W., Washington, D.C. 20036.

Advocacy Groups

These organizations are usually the result of a group of dedicated persons like yourself who have met together to form an association. Although the primary purpose of these organizations usually is advocacy, their interests and activities can be as broad as rehabilitation, education, job development and job placement. In fact, many of these organizations, such as the National Multiple Sclerosis Society and the National Association for Retarded Citizens, perceiving the need, have made combatting prejudice against the disabled in the job market a major commitment. Joining with these organizations can often lead to job offers within the organizations or through their placement services. Often you will find they have publications in which you can list a "position wanted" ad.

Rehabilitation Services

Many organizations are now combining their rehabilitation services with job development and placement. In New York City, organizations such as ICD (Institute for the Crippled and Disabled) has an active staff involved in rehabilitating individuals for jobs in the market place. The National Federation of the Blind has established JOB—Job Opportunities for the Blind—a nationwide computerized job bank for the blind. The largest organization in the field of rehabilitation, the National Rehabilitation Association, 1522 K Street, N.W., Room 1120, Washington, D.C. 20005, publishes a newsletter and holds conventions and meetings at the national, regional and local levels. Some of the offices of vocational rehabilitation are developing their own job placement facilities. The National Association of Jewish Vocational Services, with offices throughout the nation, combines rehabilitation services with placement. Handicapped individuals of all creeds are welcome to use their services. The strength of these services is illustrated through the work of the Federation of Guidance and Employment Services in New York City, which last year helped some seventy thousand individuals in rehabilitation, guidance and placement.

Veterans Organizations

Information about services to veterans is available from a number of organizations, many of which have local as well as regional offices. Foremost is the Veterans Administration, which through its local veterans assistance centers provides information on benefits, rehabilitation, counseling and job sources. Other veteran organizations include AMVETS, the Blinded Veterans Association, Disabled American Veterans, the American Legion, Veterans of Foreign Wars, Paralyzed Veterans of America, and National Association of Concerned Veterans.

College Placement Office

Don't overlook your placement officer at school or college. Each college receiving funds from the federal government must have an affirmative action program. Many of the colleges extend their affirmative action activities to the placement and referral sector. Don't be discouraged if the officer cannot place you immediately upon graduation. At your request, the college will keep your vita on file and advise you of job opportunities as they occur. They will also send your vita to interested sources. It is especially important for you to update your vita and maintain your standing with this office since specialized jobs are often funneled through the college placement officer, who then examines the vitae of the persons on file and notifies those persons whose backgrounds are most compatible with the job request. Colleges and universities take special pride in keeping track of the progress and successes of their alumnae.

Chamber of Commerce

Your local chamber of commerce can be extremely helpful in your job search. It can supply you with a list of all the companies in your area. This list can be used both for your direct mail campaign and for organizational purposes. The chamber of commerce may also be involved with or aware of job openings in your area.

Job Banks

A number of private sector training, placement projects and employment programs are sponsored by organizations. These projects may emanate from business, unions, educational institutions or organizations. They provide a sort of job bank, where a person may be trained for a job and eventually find a job through the job development resources attached to the project. In some cases, emphasis is on training, in others on placement.

Trade Journals

Depending upon the nature of the organization or business, an independent trade journal may be published by one of the business publishing organizations. These trade journals, geared to an industry, are an important source of information to members of that industry. Anyone doing business in a particular industry is certain to subscribe to a trade journal, whether the industry deals in candy manufacturing or nuts and bolts. In these trade journals, the unique needs of each industry are analyzed by a staff of experts in the field. The journals may be published weekly, monthly, bimonthly or semimonthly, and are of interest only to members of the industry concerned with the specific product. If you have training in a particular industry, you might want to take advantage of the trade journal in that field, both for sources of jobs and placement of your own ads.

Business Publications

The business newspapers and magazines cover a wider range of activities than the trade journals. Publications in the nature of *The Journal of Commerce* and *Business Week* might be a good source for higher level positions but placing your own ad would probably be prohibitively expensive.

Private Industry Councils

A number of jobs can be located through the private industry councils, a group of organizations that receive federal, state and local government funding. These councils exist in all the large cities and/or counties in the nation. They are primarily concerned with locating companies that need trained personnel for which a shortage exists in that area. The councils provide this personnel through a combination of on-the-job-training, classroom and vocational studies. Although they are not specifically set up for the handicapped population, one of their objectives is finding employment for persons with disabilities. The unique feature about this organization is that the match between you and the job may not be readily apparent, but if you are willing to train for a job that exists, you are assured of placement.

Projects with Industry

Projects With Industry (PWI) helps mentally restored people to enter the competitive labor market. New York City's Fountain House and Topeka's Menninger Clinic stress transitional employment. Other programs exist within the mental health community. Check your Department of Mental Health for more details.

On-the-Job Training

Many large corporations offer work experience programs for the handicapped. IBM for one is proud of its program, run in conjunction with the National Technical Institute for the Deaf and Gallaudet College. The corporation is also involved in training severely handicapped persons as entry-level computer programmers. More information on these programs can be obtained from your Office of Vocational Rehabilitation and the state employment offices.

Government Jobs

Consider the many possibilities of local, county, state and federal jobs. The federal government is the largest employer in the country. It is estimated that presently one out of four employed Americans has a government job. The range of offerings covers the entire spectrum of jobs found on the open market, and then some. Doctors, attorneys, accountants, market researchers, secretaries, teachers, mail clerks, surveyors, engineers, gardeners, chauffeurs—think of a job classification and rest assured that there is a governmental equivalent. Many people feel that government jobs offer greater security (and in many cases they do), the best health plans, the most liberal vacations, and the most extensive retirement plans.

In most instances, however, assignment to a particular job is based upon your ability to meet preset requirements. Civil service examinations are regularly posted. To take these examinations you must meet educational and experiential requirements. The examination is both determinative and competitive; that is, you must achieve a certain grade in order to be eligible. If there is more than one job available, your chance of getting one of these jobs will depend upon your rank as determined by the examination.

Examinations may pose a problem for you depending upon the nature of your handicapping condition. Section 501 addresses this problem directly, in the form of providing testing modifications, as follows:

Blind or Visually Impaired

Tests may be taken in braille, large print or by tape recording; the abacus may be used for mathematical computations; examiners should be available to read directions and questions and mark answer sheets; and if necessary you may be tested individually. Modified versions of the qualifying examinations and recorded test announcements and sample questions are available from any center where you will be applying.

Deaf or Hearing-Impaired

A sign language interpreter should be available to explain test procedures and directions for taking tests; if necessary, the verbal portion of some tests can be waived. You may apply for individual testing and may take modified versions of the tests.

Poor Dexterity or Coordination

Time limits are extended; answer sheets have enlarged marking blocks; examiners are available to turn pages and mark the answer sheets. You may also apply for individual testing.

In general, persons with specific handicaps usually fall into these three broad categories. For example, if you have cerebral palsy, you would fall into the poor dexterity category, if you are dyslexic, the visually impaired.

If you are not able to handle the testing situation even with the modifications, the federal government has set up a temporary trial appointment. Physically handicapped and mentally restored persons can be employed under various temporary trial appointments, the most popular of which last seven hundred hours. If you fall into this category and successfully demonstrate your ability to do the job, your temporary trial appointment can be converted to a continuing appointment. If you are mentally restored, this appointment becomes competitive; if physically handicapped, you still have the option of the competitive or excepted category.

If you are retarded, you may be excepted if you are certified as employable by a vocational rehabilitation counselor. The certification substitutes for competitive examination.

Should you take a test with or without the modifications and still not score high enough to fill one of the immediate openings, you may still be eligible for subsequent openings. Usually each "class" taking the examination retains its eligibility for a certain period of time, and during that time, no additional examinations are given. Customarily, examinations are given every six months, every year, or every two or three years. As a rule, if you are still interested in a position when an examination occurs again, you must retake it to determine your eligibility.

If you are interested in government employment, it is important to survey both the immediate offerings and those that may be listed in the near future. Since there is no single office that takes care of city, state, county and federal positions, it will be necessary for you to consult each agency individually. Further information about your rights to a job of your choice with the federal government can be had by writing to or visiting one of the local offices of personnel management (see Appendix V for listing) or writing to the Federal Civil Service Commission, Washington, D.C. Ask to be put on the mailing list so that you will received notification of the availability of federal jobs here and abroad. Your local post office may also post a number of job listings along with notices of examination date.

Should you be interested in government work, stay with it. Read all the literature available—your local library is a good source. Take whatever tests fall within your level of experience and expertise. The government often offers opportunities when all else fails, and it is likely that you will be rewarded for your persistence.

On the municipal level, check with your city or town hall; for county employment, call your county office; for state employment, consult the phone book to determine if the State Civil Service Commission has an office near your location. If not, write to the State Civil Service Commission in your state's capital requesting a list of current examinations and job openings. Ask to be put on the regular mailing list.

Register with Employment Agencies

All organizations involved in job development, whether they are private, sponsored by an organization or financed by the government, are equipped to help you find a job. It is their business. Agencies in general devote a good percentage of their time to job development. Consequently they are in a position to offer you a wider selection of jobs than you might be able to commandeer through your own efforts.

Private Employment Agencies

Applying to an agency is equivalent to applying for a number and variety of jobs. The placement manager or counselor will describe those openings for which you are qualified and which best suit your needs. Although you may have been attracted to the agency because of the advertisement of a particular job, the counselor may propose a number of other jobs that are closer to your qualifications. You need not accept any of the recommendations. You decide which of the jobs is of interest and the counselor will then make a referral. If none of the jobs is suitable, the counselor will keep your application on file and contact you when openings occur. The agency, therefore, serves as a good resource for both current and future jobs. Essentially it relieves you of some of the arduous leg work in job seeking and acts as an intermediary for you.

Many private agencies charge a fee for their services. This fee may be paid by the employee, divided between the employee and the employer, reimbursed by the employer after an agreed-upon length of time or paid entirely by the employer upon the employee's acceptance of the job. Whatever the arrangement, it is important that you read the contract carefully and ask any questions regarding your obligations before you sign the contract. As with any business agreement, it is imperative that you have clear understanding of your obligations at the beginning of the relationship.

Finding the appropriate agency is an important consideration. Many agencies specialize in certain fields or professions. A quick study of the agencies' ads will reveal an agency's particular specialty. It is also important to work with a counselor who understands your potential and who can advise and counsel you on how your skills and abilities can best be marketed. A few years ago, we interviewed a young man who was generally considered "overqualified." He had taken his Ph.D. in romance languages, was bilingual in Spanish and English, and could read and write French and Italian fluently. He preferred not to teach and had, before coming to see us, examined the other possibilities consistent with his education and abilities, including the United Nations, foreign embassies and consulates, import-export firms, multinational corporations, and the like. No realistic offer had emerged. We, unfortunately, had no opening when he registered with us, but decided to call one of our clients in international law, who referred us to a large marine insurance company. And, indeed, this company was looking for an individual with our young man's qualifications. He was hired at a managerial level.

State Employment Agencies

The United States Employment Service and its affiliated state agencies operate over twenty-five hundred local offices to serve persons seeking employment and employers seeking workers. It is currently enhancing its placement capability by using computer technology to assist in matching applicants with job openings. Unlike private agencies, state employment agencies do not charge a fee. Although their function is similar to the private agency, more time may be spent on counseling, testing and outreach programs. Thus, they are in a position to refer job seekers in need of specialized training or supportive services to local, state or federal offices. They also include among their services technical assistance in identifying and resolving internal work force problems such as turnover, absenteeism and special recruitment difficulties. They are especially empowered to serve you with counseling and assistance to overcome barriers to employment that are unrelated to job performance.

Private Nonprofit Employment Agencies

An example of a private nonprofit employment agency is Just One Break, Inc., situated in New York City. This organization provides counseling and job placement without cost to persons with handicapping conditions. Check your community for agencies patterned after this model.

The Back Door

An indirect but often successful method of landing a job is through temporary work. Although agencies dealing in temporary services do not consider themselves purveyors of jobs, their rate of placement is high. Nonprofit organizations and rehabilitation agencies also suggest temporary service as a good means for gaining entry into a company.

Look at it this way: Of the most marketable skills in the business community, typing appears to claim the honor. Typing and temporary service are almost synonymous, for although there are a number of other kinds of temporary work, the most frequent request is for a typist. Temporary service actually serves a most useful function. It provides a means of supporting yourself throughout your job search. It keeps you in the marketplace, constantly honing your skills, meeting people and proving both to yourself and to others that you are capable of performing a job. And it provides an opportunity for you to get to know an organization and for that organization to get to know you. You're "Johnny on the spot," when an opening occurs. It also tells the employer that even though you have a disability, you are in no way "dis-abled" on the job. Gordon H., plagued with a stuttering disability, is a case in point. Hired for the summer, Gordon so won the admiration and esteem of his fellow workers and supervisor that a permanent position was created for him. Gerald K., an out-of-work copywriter, took a job as a typist in an engineering firm just to tide himself over. When the company needed an editor for its house organ, Gerald stepped in. Mary

G., a crackerjack typist confined to a wheelchair, now functions as an executive secretary. Minor adaptations were all she needed to perform at full efficiency.

Classified Ads Can Tell You a Lot

The most important purpose of reading the classified advertisements is, of course, to locate a job. In addition, ads serve as a barometer of the market, general salary expectations and general availability of jobs. There is an art to reading a want ad that entails your discerning from the job description whether the company or agency is looking for a person with your qualifications.

Read ads carefully. Many of the same kinds of jobs are listed under different titles. Bookkeepers may be found under accountants; administrative secretaries under executive secretaries or administrative assistants. An editorial assistant may masquerade as a gal/guy Friday or publishing assistant. Be aware that the title of a job can at times mask the content of a job. Therefore, read the "specs" carefully. The title or classification may be simply government, union or management policy and have little to do with the actual nature of the job. In a tight job market titles may be selected to intrigue rather than reveal the essence of a job.

Use classified ads as a barometer to research of the job market. If you are not planning to look for work immediately, but want to gain insight into the kinds of jobs that are generally available, want ads can be an excellent source of information. Five columns of ads for engineers, three for typists, two for computer technologists tell you something about the trends in the labor market. A careful scrutiny of the ads over a period of months can help you determine what kinds of jobs to pursue.

You may also find that ads will help you decide if you need additional training in a particular field. You may be at the middle-management level or at the technician level and note that there is a greater number of jobs available for persons with higher skills in your particular area. Further training may enable you to take advantage of this trend.

Want ads also help you to determine realistic salary expectations. However, a word of caution here. Listed salaries are not always what they appear to be. Salaries may include the cash value of health plans, bonuses, tuition reimbursement and other company benefits. A salary difference of ten to twenty dollars in gross pay may result in only a few dollars' net pay after income tax deduction. Health plans, insurance plans and other fringes may more than adequately compensate for a lower salary level and be more desirable than a job where salary is high, but fringes are limited.

Be aware also that want ads tend to inflate or deflate salaries. Jobs carrying the same duties are often filled at salaries above or below those advertised. This variation depends upon the qualifications of the individual hired, the amount of experience, the budget line and the scarcity of personnel for the position. If fifty people apply for the same job and ten have comparable experience, the employer will probably start a person at the bottom or middle salary range, but if personnel is scarce, top dollars will be offered.

It is also wise to balance salary offered with salary potential. Accepting a lower salary than your absolute minimum with a company in the process of expansion can be more productive than holding out for the salary you had in mind with a more static organization. At times, it may be necessary to accept a lower salary if training or retraining is involved. Flexibility in salary requirements has often been the turning point in getting or losing a job.

Lastly, you will want to pursue ads to check out job availability. Do jobs exist in your area? The classified columns will tell you where jobs are located. A temporary setback in one industry, a growth spurt in another will be reflected immediately in the want-ad columns.

Direct Mail Campaign

You cannot claim to have covered all aspects of your job search if you neglect to conduct a direct mail campaign. Obviously your resume is an integral part of this campaign, and when you have prepared the best possible resume, you are ready to begin. First, compile a list of companies and organizations that interest you and that might have openings for a person with your qualifications. If you want to work where you live or within commuting distance, investigate the Yellow Pages of your local telephone directory.

Second, refer to directories such as *Standard and Poor's, Dun & Bradstreet's Million Dollar Directory and Middle Market Directory, Fortune Magazine's 500, Moody's Industrial Manual, Thomas Register of American Manufacturers,* and those of the national trade and professional associations of the United States and Canada and labor unions. If the abundance of directories appears to be overwhelming, consult *Klein's Guide to American Directories* or discuss your objectives with your neighborhood librarian. Depending upon the size of your library, a goodly number of directories should be available. Colleges that have a business administration department also house a number of directories in their libraries. If you live in a large city, the main public library should have a supply of directories to accommodate your needs. As a rule you are not allowed to withdraw directories, but will have to prepare your list in the library. However, you will probably find that you need additional information as you go along, and working in the library should not prove to be a hardship. Keep the list within reasonable limits. A long list will involve you in an interminable project that will be both discouraging and expensive.

Third, develop a covering letter (chapter 6) that can be adapted to each organization. Be sure to record the name, title of the person you want to write to, and the nature of the company's or organization's work in order to target your covering letters effectively.

Fourth, mail your letters, and within a week follow up with a telephone call. Don't wait for the organization to call you. Take the initiative. Request an interview. More than likely, even if the company does not have an opening, they will be impressed with your determination and afford you the courtesy of a meeting.

6

PLAN YOUR PAPER IMAGE: RESUMES AND LETTERS

Putting yourself on paper may well be one of the most difficult tasks facing you in your job search. How is it possible to encapsulate your three-dimensional self, your interests, hopes, aspirations and abilities on a piece of $8\frac{1}{2}$ by 11 paper? As clever as you are with words, as much help as you receive from professional and private sources, the essential *you* is hard to define. As a person with a disability, you are also troubled about whether to put information about your handicap on your resume, include it in your covering letter, or wait until you have an appointment to reveal it.

Planning the Resume

Granted that this sheet of paper cannot possibly reveal the many facets that compose the total you, what then is its purpose? Primarily, in this complex world, where distance, time and sheer numbers of individuals mitigate against personal involvement between employer and future employee for every job, the resume has been adopted as a facsimile of you, and because it must represent you when you cannot speak for yourself, it has become a very important document.

Think of the resume as your agent, your deputy, your emissary, your proxy, your go-between—in other words, that which represents you. But it needs to represent you in a certain way. Depending upon the job, it may arrive along with a heap of other resumes, all representing individuals. The greater the number of resumes, the less time each resume is given. First readers of resumes are often secretaries instructed to select only those resumes that meet the basic requirements of the job. To facilitate construction of your resume, take a look at the following rules.

Rule #1

When answering a specific ad, make sure that your resume includes information relevant to the job advertised.

The secretary may have a little more time than does the boss and may well take the trouble to ferret out those resumes that zero in and are also tangential to the job. This group of resumes is then placed in the "in" basket. The boss in moments of free time scans each resume to get an overview of the qualifications of the candidates. Since time is limited, chances are that resumes that are targeted to specific jobs will receive the most attention.

Rule #2

Write clearly and concisely. Write enough, but not too much. Limit yourself to two pages if possible.

Certain resumes may be discarded immediately, even though the content is on target. The information is disorganized. The resume is too wordy. It sounds like a number of other resumes (a problem that develops when you have a professional resume writer do your resume). Be sure your resume states exactly what you have done, can do and will be equipped to do.

Rule #3

Type your resume carefully. Be sure it is grammatically correct and does not contain spelling errors.

What makes a prospective employer turn down a resume? Well, it's not dressed well. It's sloppy. There are misspellings. There are grammatical errors. It's typed on poor paper. The copy is placed unattractively on the page. Some of the images you conjured up by a resume that falls into this category include: updating simply by writing in new information (lazy); misspelled words (careless); typographical errors (sloppy); grammatical errors (incompetent); and carelessly typed, uneven margins (uncaring).

Rule #4

Have another person proofread your resume.

Organizing Your Resume

Now that you know the resume is your representative, what do you want it to do for you? Get you the job or the interview, of course. What should it say? Just enough to tell your prospective employer what you have done in terms of education and job history. The you that goes down on paper can be divided into three categories: identifying material; work history; educational background.

The order depends upon the amount of experience you've had. Identifying information seems to work best at the beginning. If you are fresh out of school with little or no experience, you will want to place your educational background first and your work history second. If you have had a great deal of experience, your work history should be first, in reverse chronological order, that is, starting with your most recent job first. Other information, such as publications, membership in organizations and associations, if you want them on your resume, are best placed at the end. Each section should therefore contain:

- Identifying information: name, address, telephone number.

- Educational background: High school if you are a recent graduate; junior/senior colleges, date graduated, degree; vocational school, certificates or courses, dates completed; graduate school, date graduated, degree, postgraduate courses.

- Work history: Beginning with current job and working back to graduation from your most recent school, sequentially list the jobs you have held; your position and the responsibilities you have carried in each position.

To recapitulate, your resume must identify and describe you. It must include:

> your name, address and telephone number
>
> description of your educational background
>
> description of your work history
>
> honors, citations
>
> licenses that you hold
>
> membership in organizations, associations
>
> publications, if any

It may also include:

> personal data such as marital status, number of children, age, weight, height
>
> job objective or career goal
>
> brief personal history
>
> capsule description of work history
>
> information about your hobbies, interests
>
> information on your willingness to travel or relocate
>
> military or draft status
>
> statement of health

Do not include:

reasons for leaving past jobs

past salary or present salary requirements

a photograph of yourself

names of spouse and/or children

names and addresses of references

information on your disability (you are applying for the job based on your qualifications; your disability is incidental to what you can do)

Styling

In writing a resume you may choose from several different styles. These styles loosely fall into the categories of historical or chronological, functional, analytical, synoptic/amplified, and imaginative, creative or informal. Briefly, each of these styles is merely a rearrangement of the facts to emphasize an approach that is consistent with your needs and background. Let's take a look at what each of these approaches actually does.

Historical or Chronological

This approach, the most commonly used, gives a brief history of you stated in chronological terms. Your work history is presented in inverse chronological order, starting with the present or most recent experience and moving backwards in time through each datum. Dates are also included. They can be displayed in a vertical column set apart from the other information, put on a line before the pertinent information, or included as an integral part of each paragraph of your work history.

Your educational history is treated in the same manner. Your most advanced degree is stated first, followed in inverse order by all other degrees and certificates. Academic honors would be included in this grouping.

In general, emphasize those talents and abilities that are your most saleable assets. If you completed your degree at night while working on a full-time job, include this information.

The chronological resume offers a clear, concise picture of you and is one of the easiest resumes to assimilate in a quick reading. Most employers seem to prefer this type of resume, so when in doubt, go chronological.

Functional

Over the past few years the functional resume has gained in popularity, primarily because it reveals on first reading the kinds of jobs within your capacity. This resume is particularly good for persons who although they have been in the same kind of work over a number of years have moved up the career ladder. The use of this style will enable you to demonstrate your ability for assuming work under a number of different job titles. In this resume, you place the significant functions and responsibilities first. Each job title is then followed by a brief description of duties and expertise. Dates are not necessarily given, but may be included in a brief summary at the end of the narrative. We suggest a sequential job history, however brief, to assure the reader that nothing has been deleted and that no periods of time have been overlooked. The body of information in this resume is followed and concluded by your personal data.

Analytical

This approach—is similar to the functional—except that the emphasis is on talents and skills rather than job titles, which may cross over a number of jobs and educational experiences. Since these talents and skills, as in the functional resume, have been exercised on a number of jobs, the sequence of job history is sacrificed to the emphasis on ability. This type of resume, too, is ideally suited for persons who may have worked in the same type of job or in a specialized occupation for a number of years, but within that occupation have handled a variety of tasks. Here again we strongly advise giving a short chronological history of your job experience.

Synoptic/Amplified

The synoptic/amplified approach is, as its title implies, a more expansive form. On the first page, all pertinent data such as identifying information, job objective, chronological history of employment with dates, educational history and personal data are listed. The succeeding pages repeat the employment data, expanding it to include a short narrative as to the exact nature of your duties and responsibilities for each listing. Usually this resume is effective when your duties and responsibilities encompass more than the job title implies, and also when your work experience has been a long and varied one. It's disadvantage lies in the fact that it may run on for several pages, taxing the reader's time limits.

Imaginative/Creative

Creativity judiciously used can be the means to shake your resume loose from the pack. The creative approach, using art or literary techniques, may well indicate your originality but not necessarily your ability to do the job. Important here, as with the other approaches, is that the necessary information, that is, identifying information, educational and work experience, be easily accessible. A possible employer, although amused and charmed by your approach, will still want to know what you can do, what you have done, and how you went about learning to do it.

We are not downplaying creativity or originality. Rather, what we do want to stress is that you use it to enhance your resume, not overwhelm it. Different type faces make a resume easier to read and call attention to key facts. Different grades of paper, colored inks, attractive layouts all help to enhance your image. A creative approach combined with one of the more standard approaches previously described will often result in an attractive resume package.

To Tell or Not to Tell

Although you are not required to state your age, marital status, religious beliefs, race or even your sex on a resume, there are some business advisers who recommend that the more personal information is included in the resume, the greater the opportunity for an interview. A complete resume which includes all personal data helps a company fulfill its obligations of equal opportunity. Although a company may not necessarily discriminate, the Office of Equal Employment Opportunity periodically seeks information on the number of employees of various races and handicapping conditions working for a company. Large companies also put all pertinent information about an employee into their computers, and when new openings occur, run a computer search in order to give their employees an equal opportunity to compete for the job. If pertinent information is missing from your background, you might lose the opportunity for advancement.

From our experience in the field, however, and from discussions with agencies and organizations dealing with the disabled, we feel your resume should not include information about your disability. What you are selling are your skills, aptitudes and talent to perform successfully on a job. You are not marketing your handicap. A resume should state, therefore, what you can do, how well you can do it, and what you want to do, along with substantiating information. However, if you feel strongly about including the nature of your disability, by all means do so. Compliance with the laws requires that persons with handicapping conditions be given the same consideration as the general population. You just may have those qualifications necessary to help an agency or business comply with affirmative action. (Note: For a more thorough treatment on writing resumes, consult *How to Write Better Resumes,* by Adele Lewis, published by Barron's Educational Series, Woodbury, New York.)

The Introductory Letter

There will be occasions when it is more appropriate to send an introductory letter before sending along your detailed resume. You may have recently graduated from school and, therefore, have little to report in terms of real work experience. You may have been advised by a friend or associate to write a letter to an individual requesting an interview. You may be returning to work after a long period of rehabilitation or you may be reentering the job market, having spent a number of years as a homemaker. The introductory letter in these cases outlines informally what you can do, what you have done in school, at home, in volunteer activities or in retraining and suggests what you can do for the organization to which you have made application (see sample letter at end of this chapter).

The Covering Letter

The covering letter is an important document. It should be brief, written in a conversational tone, indicating why you feel that your qualifications will interest the organization. Since you are enclosing a resume giving a detailed description of your work history and skills, there is no need to repeat this information in the letter. Brevity is the key in the covering letter. It should not exceed four paragraphs. Its primary purpose is to personalize your job search. Whether you are answering an advertisement in a newspaper, sending your resume along at the suggestion of a friend, or conducting your own direct mail campaign, the covering letter is your method of informing the organization that you have the necessary skills to do that particular job.

The format of the covering letter follows standard procedure. If you do not have the name of an individual to whom to write your salutation may be Dear Sir or Madam or Dear Personnel Manager. Your opening paragraph should contain your reason for writing the letter (see samples). For the direct mail approach particularly you will want your opening sentence to state the reason you feel that this particular company can benefit from the use of your talents and experience. Composing and typing a quantity of individual letters may be time-consuming, but this extra effort is usually what makes a direct mail campaign effective.

In your middle paragraphs you will want to restate some of your work history that is relevant to the position for which you are applying. Since your resume has, in all likelihood, been reproduced in multiple copies, drawing attention to several of its features and expanding on those areas relating to the job in question are excellent means for keying the resume contents to the job in question.

Depending upon your previous experience, you may want to mention your disability. If you do not need any adaptive equipment or modification of the workplace, be sure to include this information. If your disability is invisible and you have been able to compensate for it, there is no need to mention it. Many of us function quite well with a variety of disabilities. If you need a barrier-free location, it is best to mention this fact in your covering letter. Although every organization doing business with the government must make its premises accessible to you, you will still find a number of areas, especially those not heavily trafficked, that do not conform to accessibility standards.

Your final statement should include information that you will call in a few days to arrange an interview. It is important that you take the initiative. If you wait for someone at the organization to call, you may find yourself sitting glumly by a phone that never rings. You'll feel better knowing whether or not you're succeeding in that crucial step—arranging for the interview.

Finally, the covering letter should be typed. You may reproduce resumes, but do not reproduce the covering letter. Use letterhead or 8½ by 11 bond paper. Allow sufficient margin space for an attractive appearance. Proofread each letter carefully before signing and sending it out. Typographical and spelling errors can lose you the opportunity for an interview. Remember, your letter and resume are representatives of you. A first impression is often based on these two documents.

Follow-Up Letters

A thank-you note or letter is essential to postinterview strategy. You will want to thank the person who referred you to the job, letting him or her know how much you appreciated the effort. You may also want to thank your counselor. Primarily, however, you will want to thank the personnel manager or whoever it is that interviewed you (see sample letters).

Confirmation Acceptance

Too often a verbal confirmation of an acceptance appears to suffice. But there may be an interim period between the time when you accept the job and start working. It is wise to confirm your acceptance by letter, stating the exact date when you will be starting (see sample letter).

Letter of Refusal

Thank you, no. As luck will have it, you are offered two jobs and must, therefore, decline one offer. This thank-you note is actually a public relations ploy. You never know when you might be petitioning to work for the organization in the future. It is best to be honest, straightforward and leave the door open. Take a look at the sample letter declining job offers.

PATRICIA BARNETT KARLSEN

What strikes one most forcibly about Patricia Karlsen is her indomitable spirit. Her grit was revealed in both her conversation and her actions, an example of which is the use of New York City's subway system for daily transportation—a feat she accomplishes with the aid of a rolling walker that enables her to have mobility despite impaired motor functioning as a result of cerebral palsy.

For the past twenty years, Patricia has been involved in a number of interesting and exciting assignments. At Adelphi University, where she received her B.A., she became a graduate assistant in sociology. For the next sixteen years, she was a research assistant, counselor, teacher, group leader, selection and placement officer for VISTA, and a consumer education specialist. Eight of those years was spent as a learning disabilities specialist with the United Cerebral Palsy Association of New York.

The interesting thing about Patricia's career is that she has sought jobs that challenge rather than jobs that are secure. She might have remained with United Cerebral Palsy of N.Y.C., but chose instead to trade off security for growth in skills when she accepted the job of Congress Liaison for the 1980 World Congress of Rehabilitation International. This conference drew five thousand people from all over the world. They attended eighty-three sessions, listened to three hundred speakers, and ate, slept and drank in the city of Winnipeg. With the exception of individual housing, Patricia Karlsen coordinated the scientific program activity on site.

Accommodation to the work place comes easily to Patricia. Since her marriage in 1976, when her husband insisted she learn to use the subway system, Patricia's mobility problems have been virtually nonexistent. In an office she is able to type with a specially equipped IBM electric typewriter, allowing her access to written communication.

What words of advice does Patricia Karlsen have to offer job seekers? For the teenager beginning to consider a career, she suggests that the first question should be not "what do you think you can do," but "what is it you want to do?" Once the goal has been established, Patricia sees no reason why it cannot be fulfilled. She is also a firm believer in personalizing and highlighting specific aspects of one's resume in a covering letter. She suggests a judicious use of personal contacts, but most of all, she insists that there is no substitute for persistence. "There are jobs out there," Patricia avers, "all one needs to do is make the right connections to them."

MODEL RESUME—CHRONOLOGICAL

Janet Nelson
34 Granite View
San Mateo, California 94306

Home Phone: 805-686-3240
Business: 805-322-4466

WORK EXPERIENCE:

1977 to present: Conference and Banquet Manager
                        Hotel Belvedere
                        San Mateo, Calif.

   Primarily involved in the planning and
   implementing of all conference, reception and
   banquet functions. These activities include:
   arranging suitable space to house conferences,
   receptions and banquets; developing a series of
   menus suitable for each occasion; acting as
   liaison between the hotel staff and the client to
   assure that each function runs smoothly; arranging
   entertainment at the client's request; and direct
   supervision of six employees.

   A second and equally important activity is the
   preparation of sales promotional literature
   describing the above services.

   A third element of this position is the
   development of an aggressive sales campaign that
   has resulted in a threefold increase in business.

1975-1977:   Manager
                        The Browser
                        Main Street
                        San Mateo, Calif.

   Rose from sales clerk to managerial position with
   this company. Instituted a direct mail-order
   system, set up a juvenile annex, arranged for
   weekly poetry readings, developed a Juvenile Read-
   In Promotion and organized a "Small Fry Book
   Club." As a result of these promotional
   activities, sales increased tenfold. Supervised
   four sales clerks.

1974-1975:   Administrative Assistant
                            San Mateo College
                            San Mateo, Calif.

Participated in a work-study program while
attending college. In this position, handled all
correspondence for the Dean of Student Affairs. My
duties also included the production of a four-page
newsletter, and the arrangement for a banquet for
one hundred guests.

EDUCATION: B.A., 1975 Major: English; minor: journalism
                            San Mateo College
                            San Mateo, Calif.
                            Dean's List: 1973, 1974

PERSONAL: Born: 6/7/54
                Single
                Will relocate

References available on request.

MODEL RESUME—FUNCTIONAL

Janet Nelson   Home Phone: 805-686-3240
34 Granite View   Business Phone: 805-322-4466
San Mateo, California 94306

Job Objective: A position as Conference Manager.

WORK HISTORY:

Conference and Banquet Manager:

Developed extensive sales promotional activities to
attract attention to the conference facilities at the
Hotel Belvedere, San Mateo. As a result of these
promotional campaigns, bookings increased threefold.
Organized, developed and trained staff to handle
banquet, reception and conference programs. Instituted
the concept of "custom-made" affairs to provide clients
with an individually planned program to meet their
specific needs.

Book Store Manager:

Instituted a comprehensive direct-mail-order system to
increase the sales of specialized books. Set up a
juvenile annex where young people were encouraged to
browse. Developed a "Small Fry Book Club" for children
aged 5 to 7. Arranged to rent space in an adjoining
building that we named "Book Space." Weekly poetry ·
readings, Saturday story hours and Sunday concerts were
held in that area.

Administrative Assistant:

Handled all correspondence for the Dean of Student
Affairs at San Mateo College. Produced a four-page
newsletter. Made all the arrangements for a banquet
serving one hundred guests.

JOB HISTORY:

              1977 to present: Conference and Banquet Manager
                                  Hotel Belvedere
                                  San Mateo, Calif.

```
1975-1977:              Manager
                        The Browser
                        Main Street
                        San Mateo, Calif.

1974-1975:              Administrative Assistant
                        San Mateo College
                        San Mateo, Calif.
```

EDUCATION:

```
     B.A., 1975         San Mateo College
                        San Mateo, Calif.

                        Major: English
                        Minor: Journalism

                        Participated in work-study
                          program, 1974-75.
                        Dean's List: 1973, 1974.
```

PERSONAL:

```
                        Date of birth: 6/7/54
                        Single
                        Will relocate
```

References available on request.

MODEL RESUME—ANALYTIC

Janet Nelson   Home Phone: 805–686–3240
34 Granite View   Business Phone: 805–322–4466
San Mateo, California 94306

Job Objective: Application of my past experience to the
position of Conference Manager.

Qualifications:

Managerial Skills: In the capacity of Conference
and Banquet Manager of the largest hotel in San
Mateo, I am fully responsible for both the
administrative functions and promotional aspects
of the entire operation. This includes: budget
preparation, space arrangement, menu selection,
client contact and supervision of personnel.

As Bookstore Manager, I was responsible for all
administrative functions relating to the sales
promotion department.

Sales Promotional Skills: Developed an energetic
sales promotion campaign to bring the Belvedere
Hotel to the attention of organizations seeking
sites for national conventions. Features of this
program included the writing and production of
sales promotional literature, development of a
mailing list, and personal contact with presidents
of trade and nonprofit organizations about the
advantages of holding their annual conventions in
San Mateo. The results of these efforts increased
sales threefold.

Organized a local arts program to increase book
sales at The Browser Book Store. This program
included weekly poetry readings, Saturday story
hours, Sunday concerts, a "Small Fry Book Club"
for children aged 5 to 7, and a juvenile annex for
young people. Developed a comprehensive direct-
mail–order system to increase the sales of
specialized books. Business increased tenfold
during my period of employment with this concern.

Supervisory Skills: In my last two positions, I
have supervised from five to seven employees. The
nature of this supervision has been broad and
varied, ranging from book-store employees to
copywriters to hotel employees.

EMPLOYERS:

1977 to present: Conference and Banquet Manager
                    Hotel Belvedere
                    San Mateo, California

1975-1977:   Manager
                    The Browser
                    Main Street
                    San Mateo, Calif.

1974-1975:   Administrative Assistant
                    San Mateo College
                    San Mateo, California

EDUCATION:

B.A., 1975   San Mateo College
                    San Mateo, Calif.

                    Major: English
                    Minor: Journalism

                    Participated in work-study
                      program, 1974-75.

                    Dean's List: 1973, 1974.

PERSONAL:

Date of birth: 6/7/54
Single
Will relocate

References available on request

MODEL RESUME—SYNOPTIC/AMPLIFIED

Janet Nelson   Home Phone: 805-686-3240
34 Granite View   Business Phone: 805-322-4466
San Mateo, California 94306

WORK EXPERIENCE:

1977 to present: Conference and Banquet Manager
                    Hotel Belvedere
                    San Mateo, Calif.

1975-1977:   Manager
                    The Browser
                    Main Street
                    San Mateo, Calif.

1974-1975:   Administrative Assistant
                    San Mateo College
                    San Mateo, Calif.

EDUCATION:

B.A., 1975   San Mateo College
                    San Mateo, Calif.

                    Major: English
                    Minor: Journalism

                    Participated in work-study program,
                       1974-75
                    Dean's List: 1973, 1974

PERSONAL:

                    Born: 6/7/54
                    Single
                    Will relocate

For amplification, see following page.

WORK EXPERIENCE:

1977 to present: Conference and Banquet Manager:
Developed extensive sales promotional
activities to attract attention to
the conference facilities at the
Hotel Belevedere, San Mateo. As a
result of these promotional
campaigns, bookings increased
threefold. Organized, developed and
trained staff to handle banquet,
reception and conference programs.
Instituted the concept of "custom-
made" affairs to provide clients with
an individually planned program to
meet their specific needs.

1975-1977:   Manager: The Browser:
Instituted a comprehensive direct-
mail-order system to increase the
sales of specialized books. Set up a
juvenile annex where young people
were encouraged to browse. Developed
a "Small Fry Book Club" for children
aged 5 to 7. Arranged to rent space
in an adjoining building that we
named "Book Space." Weekly poetry
readings, Saturday story hours and
Sunday concerts were held in that
area.

1974-1975:   Administrative Assistant, San Mateo
College:
Handled all correspondence for the
Dean of Student Affairs at San Mateo
College. Produced a four-page
newsletter. Made all the arrangements
for a banquet serving one hundred
guests.

References can be supplied upon request.

MODEL RESUME—CREATIVE

INTERESTED IN SALES EXPANSION?

OPEN TO INNOVATIVE PLANNING?

NEED THE TOUGH COMBINATION OF MANAGERIAL AND SALES
PROMOTIONAL SKILLS?

Then let me tell you what I can do. In the past
eight years, I have been responsible for:

--Setting up a direct-mail-order system for a
medium-sized book company.

--Instituting a cultural program of poetry
readings, concerts, Saturday story telling,
book clubs, increasing business tenfold.

--Developing special book departments to attract
young people.

--Developing extensive sales promotional
activities at the Hotel Belevedere, San Mateo,
resulting in a threefold increase in bookings.

--Instituting "custom-made" affairs providing
clients with an individually planned program
to meet their specific needs.

--Writing sales promotional literature.

--Producing in-house newsletters.

--Managing two vigorous promotional departments,
one for book sales, the other for hotel
conference and banquet sales.

--Supervising a medium-sized staff of sales
clerks, copywriters and hotel employees.

I received my B.A. in English and journalism from San
Mateo College, California in 1975. Since that time I

have been actively engaged in the above promotional
activities. I am single, willing to relocate to any part
of the country, and can make arrangements for an
interview immediately upon your request.

CALL ME or WRITE TO ME: Janet Nelson, 34 Granite
View, San Mateo, California. Home phone: 805-686-
3240; business phone: 805-322-4466.

MODEL INTRODUCTORY LETTER

Mr. Barton Mosby
Cayton Machine Tool Company
210 Barrow St.
Clayton, Ohio 45315

Dear Mr. Mosby:

I have been advised by my high school guidance
counselor, Mrs. Morrison at Attlebury High School, to
write to you about a training position with your
company.

My qualifications include a year of training in the
vocational division of Attlebury High School. I worked
six months in automotive repairs, and six months in
small appliance repairs. I can read a blueprint, and
have no trouble following a schematic. Since I have been
a child, I have always been interested in machines and
tools, and I find that I am happiest when I am working
with this kind of equipment.

I must mention that I have a hearing handicap. I can
handle most communications with the aid of my amplifying
equipment, lip reading and sign language. My disability
has not affected my ability to learn, and last year I
won an award for outstanding achievement in a work-study
program.

I hope that I may have the pleasure of meeting you. I
will call you in several days to arrange for an
appointment.

                    Sincerely,

                    Richard Thomas

MODEL COVERING LETTER

EDITORIAL ASSISTANT

Music trade publication
seeks editorial assistant
experienced in writing,
copyediting and layout.
Send resume and salary
requirements to:
RR192TIMES10108

RR192
Times 10108
The New York Times
19 West 44th St.
New York, New York 10036

Dear Personnel Director:

I am replying to your advertisement for an editorial
assistant for your music trade publication. As you can
see from my resume, I graduated with a B.A. in English.
In my senior year, I was editor of the college literary
journal, Sixpence.

In addition to my experience on the Sixpence, I compose
and sing songs to my own guitar accompaniment. The job
you advertised appears to fit in perfectly with my
interests and experience.

I wish to be frank with you. Since my sixteenth
birthday, I have been confined to a wheelchair as a
result of an automobile accident. My disability has in
no way affected my capacity to hold down a job.
Transportation is no problem since I own and drive my
own car.

I would welcome the opportunity to meet with you to
discuss my qualifications for this job. In my last
position, I received $15,000 per annum. However, since I

am eager to move into the field of music publishing, I prefer to keep the question of salary open.

Thank you in advance for your consideration.

Sincerely,

Ann Jordan

MODEL LETTER—FOLLOW-UP TO PERSONNEL MANAGER

Mr. James Crossley
Strand Motor Company
25–35 Strand Way
Worcester, Massachusetts 02299

Dear Mr. Crossley:

I was especially pleased to meet with you last Wednesday. The position you described appears to match my qualifications perfectly, and I would welcome the opportunity to work for your company.

Do let me know if you require additional information or references. I shall be pleased to forward any materials upon your request. In the meantime, I hope that I may hear from you soon.

With best wishes,

Sincerely,

Arthur Berg

MODEL LETTER—FOLLOW-UP TO VOCATIONAL COUNSELOR

Mr. Ralph Jones
Vocational Services, Inc.
1421 Allerton Way
Madison, Wisconsin 53701

Dear Mr. Jones:

Thank you for referring me to Patchen Sales Company. I met with the personnel manager, who introduced me to the sales manager. The sales manager and I talked for about ten minutes. He appeared to be pleased with my qualifications and advised me that I would hear from the personnel manager within the week.

I feel confident that I can handle the job, and hope that Patchen will make me an offer. Any assistance you can offer toward helping me obtain the job will be greatly appreciated.

                    Sincerely,

                    Maria Sanchez

MODEL LETTER—FOLLOW-UP NOTE CONFIRMING REFUSAL OF JOB OFFER BUT LEAVING OPTIONS OPEN

Ms. Beverly Nippon
Oltec Sales Company
22506 Freeway
Houston, Texas 77060

Dear Ms. Nippon:

I am indeed flattered that you have offered me the job of traffic manager. Unfortunately, the offer came one week too late, for I have just this week accepted a similar job with another company. I am sorry that the timing was not propitious, since I was impressed with your organization and, had the offer been made last week, would have made it my first choice.

May I suggest, therefore, that you keep my resume on file, should my present position fail to meet my expectations. Perhaps if another opening occurs within the next year, we can reopen our discussion.

Thank you for your consideration, and again, I am sorry to refuse your offer at this time.

                    Sincerely,

                    Walter Scott

7

BANISH INTERVIEW JITTERS

The best time to go on an interview is when you have a perfectly satisfactory job, you've been sought out by a prospective employer who wants to lure you away and you're doubtful that you want to change jobs at this particular time. Psychologically, the unhooked fish becomes the most desirable. Alas, in the majority of cases, you are interviewed when you are most in need of a job—that is, when you are out of work, or when your present job is terminating. Is there any wonder, then, that the interview looms in your mind as an acid test of your ability, personality and capability. You probably alternate between being angry that you have only approximately half an hour to let the interviewer know and find out about you, and a feeling of disquietude or of wondering what else there is to say when you said it all in your resume. Added to the common fears of being interviewed are your uncommon fears about your handicapping condition. Will you be able to persuade the interviewer whom you finally confront that you can indeed do the job? You know you can do the job, or you would not have applied for it, but . . . .

Rest assured, you're in good company. Whether you're applying for your first job as a babysitter or you're halfway up the ladder in an industry, putting yourself in the "hot seat" is an unsettling experience. Our experience in the agency, and with what other placement organizations tell us, confirms the fact that the interview is one of the most stressful experiences in the job search. The interview often appears to be a series of barriers. Your first interview is with your job counselor who, as the term implies, will counsel you on the techniques of obtaining an interview. Not surprisingly, the relationship you establish with the counselor may be indicative of the number of interviews and job offers you receive. The second interview barrier is with the personnel manager or office manager. If you successfully negotiate this hurdle, the next interview should be with the person for whom you would work. In some cases, however, you may pass through several different layers of personnel in the process of interviewing. Each layer will represent a different aspect of the company or organization. All told, the waters of interviewing contain some tricky shoals.

But take heart. The fact that thousands upon thousands of people are interviewed and hired daily attests to the fact that people do get the jobs they seek. Let's look at the interview realistically. You've been called for an interview for one of several reasons: 1. your resume fits the job description; 2. your job counselor has recommended you; 3. a personal friend or acquaintance has recommended you. In all three cases something or someone has told the interviewer about you. You are there to amplify the information, give the interviewer the opportunity to see how you personally respond to questions and, not incidentally, to learn more about the job.

The Interviewer's Expectations

The interview for a person with a disability is basically no different from that of any job seeker. The interviewer and the interviewee are meeting to evaluate whether each can be of benefit to the other. Most likely, the interviewer has been made aware of your disability, either from previous correspondence with you or from your counselor. Now is the time, however, to allay fears about the effects of your disability upon your work performance. You probably have more knowledge of specific modifications or accommodations you will need to fulfill the job requirements efficiently. This information should be discussed in a straightforward manner. Feel free to ask questions about the working conditions, but keep these questions on a fact-finding level, thus allowing you the opportunity to demonstrate how you can fit into the organizational structure. Don't be taken aback if the interviewer asks questions about your disability, questions that do not seem to be job-related. He or she may be seeking information on how you may react to questions posed by your future fellow employees.

If you sense that your interviewer is uneasy in your presence, it may be wise to put him or her at ease about your disability. Talk freely about what you can or cannot do. Allow your interests, ideas and projections to narrow the gap between "disabled" and "abled." Chances are that when the interviewer realizes that major differences do not exist between you and other candidates as a result of your disability, the interviewing climate will become more confident and accepting.

Learning as much as you can about the job before you reach the interview stage is good preparation. The more you know, the better you will be able to field questions about how you can fit into the organization. An interviewer is often interested in your reaction to a job description, company policy or products. You may be interviewing for a job with a firm that among its subsidiaries produces chemicals harmful to the environment. You are an environmentalist. Can you justify working for this firm even though you will not be working in the chemical division? The interviewer is also interested in other qualities that you possess, qualities that have not necessarily shown up on your resume. There is that magical word, *chemistry*. Does your chemistry blend in with the company? In places where both authors of this book have worked, the only description of a suitable personality type was obsessive-compulsive. Any other personality was simply overwhelmed by the pace of the organization. Many organizations appear to have a certain image. The interviewer is interested to know if you fit the image.

While this elusive fit might dog some of your interview encounters, we strongly urge that you do not try to shape yourself into the image you think an organization projects. You can't do it. You might be able to carry off the role during the interview, but your true personality soon emerges. Be yourself. A straightforward interview is always the most impressive. Whatever else the interviewer may be looking for, his or her main concern is your integrity as an individual.

The same advice applies if you are interviewing for a job where one of the hurdles is a group interview. In many organizations, people work closely together. When a vacancy occurs, there is genuine concern on the part of the staff that the person hired fit in as a member of the team. The interviewee is therefore asked to meet with members of the staff in an informal setting. Another type of group interview might be one involving a nonprofit organization or a funded project. These organizations have boards of directors who oversee the administrative and political aspects of the organization. Depending upon its composition, the board interview may or may not be stressful.

By and large, however, you are called in for an interview primarily because you are considered a likely candidate for a job opening. The organization needs you. They have spent money recruiting you. They have talked with placement agencies, both public and private, placed advertisements, sent recruiters out to colleges in an effort to find you. You are as important to the organization as it is to you. Therefore, the interview is, indeed, bilateral. Both sides can win or lose.

Ways to Score Points

How do you score points? Provided you have the qualifications for the job, the system is remarkably easy to incorporate. And it works for anyone, whether at entry level or top management.

Be Enthusiastic

Let them know that you're really interested in the job, that it is meaningful to you to work with the organization. By enthusiastic we don't mean being overly effusive, but displaying genuine interest. Some job seekers mistakenly feel that it's best to be cool on an interview. They lower the temperature to the point where they freeze out communication. A person who is being cool is often viewed by the interviewer as apathetic, uncommunicative, bored, hostile or trying to hide something.

Be Yourself

Your own personality is the most valid one. Giving an honest representation of yourself will do a great deal toward banishing your interview jitters. If you know you will be hired based on your qualifications, you can relax and establish true rapport, an ingredient essential to a successful interview.

Be Prepared

Reread your resume. The interviewer will no doubt have a copy of your resume on his or her desk. Reference may be made to a section that needs further clarification. If you haven't looked at the resume for several months or even weeks, you might flounder, or may even leap up to read your resume over the interviewer's shoulder. Bad business. Know exactly what you have said in both your resume and covering letter. You might have sent out a dozen covering letters, each one stressing a different facet of your background, but relevant to a particular organization. Keep a carbon of the letters for easy referral.

Be Honest

Past information on previous salaries, responsibilities and job duties can boomerang if you have not honestly reported them. Even if you feel that you are worth more than you were paid in your last job, and the job which you are seeking is listed at a considerably higher salary, inflating salaries on past jobs can mean the difference between getting or losing a job, especially if this information is relayed to your prospective employer. The same holds true for responsibilities and duties. Claim competence or skills only for those jobs you have actually done.

Be honest about the reasons you are no longer employed. Chances are you have a legitimate reason for termination. Tell it like it is. If your work history is sound, one termination will not detract from the overall impression. However, if you have been terminated on all of your jobs for the same reason, it is unlikely that the employer will want to risk hiring you. You might need professional assistance to overcome workplace difficulties.

Be Tolerant: Use each interview as a learning experience

It would save all of us a great deal of anguish if we were to be slotted into jobs without the fuss of comparison and contrast with a number of other applicants. Or would it? For better or worse, ours is a competitive society. And who can deny that there is something exhilarating about landing a coveted job, a big fish—winning. Getting a job is winning. To win, you need to have some experience, some training. If you don't get the job, why not look upon the experience as part of your training? When you have been on several interviews, analyze the experience, discuss it with your counselor. What can you do differently? What did you notice during the interview that worked for you? Against you? Did you really want the job or were you ambivalent about it? What more could you have done? Use each interview as a learning experience, a training ground to boost your confidence in yourself, rather than as an undermining experience of failure when you do not get the job.

Be Dressed Properly

Important! You really do need to be appropriately dressed when going on an interview. Neatness and cleanliness of body and clothes is essential. Avoid fad dressing. We're not advocating that you be primly dressed, but that your clothes reflect your concern for the company's image. Unfortunately, wonderful personal qualities are often hidden behind sloppy, casual attire. Since first impressions count, make yours a good one. Keep in mind that you will be interviewed by a human being who has his or her own quirks and prejudices. Therefore, for example, be discreet about advertising your views on controversial subjects by wearing political buttons or insignia. Mind you, we are not suggesting that you abjure your views, but merely recommend that you find a platform other than the job interview to broadcast them.

Be Thorough in Filling Out the Application Form

As distasteful as it may be, there will always be forms to fill out. It is the bane of civilization. Even though all the information is recorded on your resume, take the time to fill out the form completely. Describe your abilities, not your disabilities. Print neatly in the space allowed. Provide only those facts that accurately describe what the employer can expect of you on a particular job. You may elect to put down the nature of your disability on the application form. If you do, do not use medical terms. Describe the disability in simple terms. However, there is no requirement that you state your disability in writing. Therefore, you may choose to discuss it at the interview. If you have a hidden disability that in no way interferes with your job performance, you may choose, if you are comfortable with the choice, not to discuss or refer to the problem. The application form may also call for minimum salary requirements. If you are unsure, you can leave this space open. Some applications ask for information such as "what would you like to be doing ten years from now?" Answer directly but gear your answer as much as possible to the job for which you are applying, but to a higher level. You may also be asked why you chose this particular company. Keep your answers positive. If you really want to work for this company, here is the place to make this sentiment known.

If you are just starting your search, you might want to carry around a "pocket resume," to help you transfer information onto the application form. Your pocket resume should have the following information:

Your name, address and telephone number

Your parents' names and addresses

The date of your birth

The names, addresses and dates you graduated from the schools you've attended

The names, addresses and dates of work of any places where you've worked

Your social security number

You should also have, should you need them, working papers, a copy of your birth certificate, your draft card if you have one, and your driver's license if you have one.

Be Willing to Take a Test

You may say you can type 50 WPM, that you can run a drill press, that you can operate a machine, that you can teach a class, that you can balance a set of books. You know you can do it, but how sure is the interviewer of your competence? In many cases an interviewer is only satisfied by a demonstration of your ability. Therefore, you may be asked to take a short test. Depending upon the organization, the test may be formally or informally administered. If you need testing modifications, discuss these with the interviewer.

Some organizations feel the need to administer aptitude, intelligence and personality tests. Although we are not persuaded that these tests, unless administered by your vocational counselor, predict your capabilities better than a review of your past experience, we find it difficult to buck company policy. If this kind of testing is a prerequisite of the job, and if all future employees are also tested and you have no aversion to taking the test, go ahead. However, if the test is only required of you because of your disability, you have a right to complain of discriminatory practices. If you decide to take the test and the company or organization is an affirmative action employer, you are entitled to testing modifications (see chapter 3).

Be Positive in Your Approach

A positive attitude is considered one of the major components of a worker's ability. We hear it said again and again, especially on entry-level jobs, that it's not at all difficult to train an individual in the duties of a job. What is most difficult to control is the attitude of the individual. Let the interviewer know that you can take constructive criticism, get along with others, get along with superiors, work independently when necessary; work as part of a team when the situation calls for it; follow the rules and regulations of the company; work through the proper channels for resolution of a problem; and express company loyalty.

Don't blurt out these attributes, but in the course of talking with the interviewer indicate how you worked with a team on a certain project, solved problems, expressed company loyalty, and so on.

Clinch That Interview

Walking out the door does not complete the interview process. A job is often landed through postinterview techniques. If you are truly interested in the job, let the interviewer know through your enthusiastic follow-up procedures. The postinterview time is when you open both barrels to let the organization know that you want the job. It's no time to be coy or play hard to get. Project your enthusiasm in a letter or phone call. Don't be gushy or overly confident. Simply let them know that based on the interview and your recent exposure to the organization that you are indeed interested in working for them. Your simple thank-you letter might be the item that singles you out for the job.

Briefly, the following are some of the important points to remember as published by Just One Break, New York, N.Y.

DO

Learn about the firm and its products before applying.

Apply in person—go alone.

Be on time for appointments.

Look presentable—clean and well-groomed.

Apply for specific kind of work.

Stress your experience, training, and skills (include military).

Briefly explain your physical limitations—when asked.

Speak with confidence—give honest answers.

Make your written application neat, complete and accurate.

Give references when requested.

Listen respectfully to employer's comments or advice.

Thank employer when leaving or even better, write him a note thanking him for the interview.

DON'T

Mumble your name, fidget or slouch

Apologize for lack of experience.

Dwell on your disability.

Plead your need for work.

Argue with or antagonize employer.

Criticize former employees or associates.

Try too hard to make an impression.

Misrepresent facts, or bluff.

Conceal your disability.

Talk too much.

Assume employer owes you a job.

Be discouraged if first interview fails.

WHEN YOU'RE HIRED

Be punctual and conscientious.

Learn your job duties and perform them well.

Don't quit your job except for an excellent reason. Remember another job may be hard to find.

Obey company rules and regulations.

Cooperate with supervisors and fellow workers.

Don't expect special privileges because of your handicap.

Your successful performance on the job may make it easier for other disabled job seekers.

8

BECOME AN EXPERT JOB HUNTER

The stage is set. You have become involved in a community job campaign. You have examined the job market. You have evaluated your skills and accomplishments. You have prepared your tools—the resume and covering letters. You may even have made some attempts to find a job, practice runs, to see how you fared on interviews. But you still may not be sure that you've got it all together, that it is working for you.

What you need now is a perspective, a set of guidelines that apply only to you. Where do you belong? How does your condition affect your chances for the kind of employment you want? Can you get work in the field where you've had the most training, or will your degrees count for little? Are there alternatives that will be satisfactory? Are you riding high on myth or do you have reality firmly in rein?

How You Are Different

Are there differences between you and a nondisabled worker? Yes and no. On paper you both look alike. Your resumes cover your education, past job experience and objectives. Your job-hunting techniques are for the most part similar. You will both want to take advantage of all the same resources, including private and state employment agencies, newspaper ads, developing your own direct mail campaign. In short, you will both be planning your job-hunting strategies along the guidelines set forth in the preceding chapters.

Where you yourself differ from the nondisabled worker is in your need for accessibility and modification of the environment. However, in a sense this may give you a bit of an edge, for you can also tap private and public rehabilitation agencies for assistance and support, and you have the Rehabilitation Act of 1973 behind you in the form of affirmative action to ensure that there will be some jobs set aside especially for you.

Nevertheless, you may still feel that you are at a disadvantage. Why not turn prejudice to your advantage?

Prejudice unfortunately stems from ignorance, lack of communication, generalization from the particular to the whole, and a general lack of understanding of the causes and ramifications of the issue at hand. In essence, you are your own emissary. You are already painfully aware of the reactions of many people to your disability. Some of these reactions are similar to that of a traveler in a foreign country who, not able to speak the native language, speaks his or her own language in loud dominant tones, assuming that volume will get the message through. Unfortunately, this premise that a loud voice will ease communication seems to extend to dealings with persons who have disabilities, a factor that immediately sets up barriers to normal communication.

Communication is, in fact, the major stumbling block. How do you let a person know that you hear perfectly well although your sight, mobility or rate of learning is impaired? How do you get it across to your nondisabled colleagues that it's okay to push your wheelchair, help you get things from a high shelf, hold the elevator door while you negotiate entrance, help you up the steps or off the curb when no ramps or curb cuts exist. Many people want to help but they are afraid of offending, or even worse, they block you out, pretend you don't exist. There are other people, of course, who smother you with assistance. How do you tactfully resolve either of these two extremes? If you are blind or severely handicapped, how do you let people know when help is important and when you can manage by yourself? How can you persuade them to keep furniture in access areas in the same arrangement, or if changes are made, to inform you? How do you get it across to your colleagues that the special equipment you use is not a special dispensation but necessary for your survival in the organization? Similar problems will apply if you are deaf or severely hearing-handicapped. How do you persuade your colleagues that your disability in no way affects your performance? How do you let colleagues know that learning more slowly or learning differently does not make you incompetent? How do you persuade your co-workers that although you are mentally restored or a recovered addict, you still need to exert care for your condition. You have no obvious disability, yet you are asking for certain modifications. How do you handle the problems of dexterity when you have a physically handicapping condition, the problems of shortened hours, rest periods, irregular work schedules? How, in fact, can you handle prejudice stemming from the differences between yourself and other workers.

You talk to your co-workers, that's how. You tell them what is best for you and you ask them what is best for them. You let it be known that you understand their quirks and idiosyncrasies that are often passed off as superstitions or family traits. You don't brood over slights and lack of consideration on the part of your colleagues. Rather, you clear the air, not judgmentally, but simply by stating facts and feelings. People feel better when they can be genuinely helpful. They neither want to nurse a co-worker nor ignore one. Since you may be the only person with your particular disability at your place of work, or at the place where you are being interviewed for work, let your colleagues know your strengths and weaknesses.

Because of your particular disability, you have had good training in determining your own strengths and weaknesses. Persons without obvious disabilities know they do things well or poorly, but they seldom reflect on how their particular attributes contribute to their successes and failures. You, on the other hand, throughout your education, whether you are developmentally disabled or have been disabled as a result of an accident or disease, have been focusing on building your strengths and strengthening your weaknesses wherever possible.

In the job market your strengths will undoubtedly be your selling point. You have already analyzed some of the qualities that appear to match certain professions (chapter 2). If you find that you possess a group of these qualities, capitalize on them. Go after those particular professions or allied professions where your particular strengths can become an asset to an organization. It is important to remember that large organizations, including the Federal Government, have a range of jobs. Therefore, when you think IBM, for example, think, in addition to computers, writing, legal, accounting, sales, clerical.

It's Not Always Prejudice

Why can't I get a job? After a somewhat fruitless search, this question is echoed by every job seeker, whether or not he or she is handicapped. What's holding me back? Your first impulse, of course, is to assume that prejudice is operating. You may be right, and, indeed, it may be the reason why you are not hired. Yet other possibilities do exist. Let's examine what these may be before you leap to the conclusion that prejudice is holding you back.

Foremost in analyzing job readiness is the acquisition of skills. Do you have the skills for the job? If the job calls for a typist and you type twenty words per minute, it is not your disability but your typing speed that is holding you back. If you apply for a job as a bricklayer and you've not served the required apprenticeship, then you can't handle the job. If the job lists at least two years' experience and you are fresh out of school, you are not yet ready for this job.

By and large, when you apply for a job, whatever it is, you need skills. There are a number of jobs where the skills are readily transferrable. These jobs occur in most offices, retail businesses, restaurants, and are found in almost all of the entry-level jobs. The higher up the ladder, however, the more specialized your skills and experience. In addition, you will often find yourself honing those specialized skills to keep up with new developments in your field. In some jobs and professions the learning process never ends.

Consider your alternatives. In your job search, it is important to consider fields other than the kind of work you have been doing, at which you may have become disabled, or work that does not seem relevant to what you have studied in either high school or college. Although at first glance alternatives may seem a compromise of the ideal, carefully thought-out choices serve to widen the arc of your working potential. Basically we are not advocating that you discard your goals and ideals altogether, but that you understand that building a career requires flexibility and openness to a variety of possibilities.

Different kinds of training produce different aspirations. In our work with those of you who are liberal arts college graduates, we often find that your journey through academe has been a wonderful adventure of research, scholarship, and philosophical theorizing that has permitted you the rare opportunity to exchange your ideas with the great minds of the world, living and dead. From this rarefied atmosphere, you are thrust into the job world. If you haven't trained to a particular profession, the array of jobs can be fascinating, bewildering and, unfortunately, discouraging, since many of the entry-level jobs, even with a college degree, ask for some kind of office skill.

Nevertheless, the College Placement Council in a recent survey found that most college graduates are satisfied with their careers; those most satisfied included business administrators, salespeople, teachers and health workers. Office workers were the least satisfied of all the occupational groups surveyed. From an analysis of the responses as a whole, the council concluded that the attempt to create a perfect fit between college education and careers was a wasted effort, since once the student was out of college and in the working world, fit did not really matter. Apparently men and women who considered their jobs closely related to their major subject seemed to be no more satisfied with their work than those who strayed further afield from their college studies.

Our own experience confirms these findings. Catherine, a science major with a bent for writing, was hired as a junior copywriter in an advertising agency. Henry, an art major, became a management trainee. Susan, after training to be a dental assistant and deciding that she disliked the limitations of the profession, became a merchandising trainee and is now a buyer.

If you have not completed college, have just graduated from high school, or have no particular training, it is extremely important that you consider all possibilities. Most likely you will be in touch with your vocational counselor who will be able to offer you a number of suggestions. Openness to these suggestions is advisable. You never know where a job will lead.

You may be in the position of not being able to return to your old profession because of a work-related disability, or you may feel the need to change fields. If you have gone through a rehabilitation program, work closely with your counselor. He or she will probably be in a position to recommend satisfactory alternative jobs. Changing fields may pose little problem if you choose a field where you can use your skills. You may have developed a reputation as a sales manager for a particular industry. An allied or different industry has need of a sales manager. Although you do not know the product, your skills of communication, marketing and working with sales personnel along with your conviction that you can sell the company's product will probably persuade the employer to hire you.

Alternatives exist since each field has within it both the specialists and the generalists. In addition, within each field, there exists a variety of jobs. Thus, a nurse may work in a hospital, a school, an institution or a company. A writer may work for a newspaper, a trade magazine, in a public relations office, as a grant writer, a pamphlet writer or in an advertising agency. A person with mechanical skills may work in an apartment building, a machine shop, a repair shop or heavy or light industry. Flexibility is the keyword, whether you are a recent high school or college graduate, trainee or returnee, or simply looking to change fields.

Put It All Together

Everyone will tell you how to look for a job. Almost everyone will concur that looking for a job is as much a job as the job itself. A number of experts will purport to know exactly what you must do, how you must do it and even, for a sum of money, offer to do it for you. In our experience, however, we have found that looking for a job combines a number of different factors, and as with every human endeavor, there is a great deal of variability in the guidelines. Therefore, rather than burden you with unwieldy strategies, strict time lines, burdensome research, we are offering you the core of our experience.

- Prepare the best possible resume. Have friends, colleagues and one or two employment managers critique your resume before running off a large number of copies.

- Get to know your vocational rehabilitation counselor, your state vocational counselor, and several counselors in private agencies. Keep in touch with these counselors when they send you on jobs. Let them know the result of the interviews. If you haven't heard from them for a period of time, visit them again. The better they know you, the more apt they will be to remember you when a job request comes in.

- Be sure that each covering letter is custom-typed and directed to the advertisement to which you're responding.

- Get on the phone. You will need to do a lot of phone inquiry before you make one visit. Learn about potential employers before you meet with them. Learn everything you can about the organization. A little knowledge gained from an afternoon of research can create a bridge between you and your prospective employer.

- If the thought of an interview sends chills up your spine, practice interviewing techniques. Family, friends and counselors are generally pleased to assist in role-playing interview situations.

- Follow up, follow up, follow up. We cannot repeat this phrase often enough. Call the counselor, friends or acquaintances who arranged the interview to let them know your impressions. Send a letter to the personnel manager or future employer, thanking him or her for the interview.

- Listen carefully to the advice of your placement counselor after you've been on several interviews that did not "take." His or her suggestions for modification of your approach can be extremely valuable to you.

- Dress appropriately. NCD: neat, clean, discreet.

LINDA SLONE

Entering buildings through back loading platforms, jockeying for parking spaces close enough to her destination, maneuvering herself in and out of tight-access passageways hasn't dimmed Linda Slone's spirit in the least. In fact, the attributes one remembers about Linda are her bright smile, her willingness to do a difficult job, and her adept problem-solving ability.

Linda's smile and the determination emanating from an undaunted spirit have carried her from the time she was stricken with polio (she was in the last wave of victims before the introduction of the Salk vaccine) to her present-day role of teacher-trainer fighting for her own equal rights and thus enhancing the equal rights of others who have handicapping conditions.

Her first experience in bending rules occurred when she visited her counselor at the Office of Vocational Rehabilitation to gather information on postsecondary education and job prospects. Based upon her SAT scores, her counselor advised her against seeking entrance into a college. Linda knew her SATs did not accurately reflect her ability, but rather than attempt to dissuade her counselor, she researched colleges on her own time, and came up with an institution that would accept her, probationally, provided she pulled at least a B for two consecutive terms. Linda made the Dean's list.

From that point on, Linda experienced little trouble gaining her goals. Using a wheelchair for mobility, Linda set out to attain her objectives. She graduated with an M.S. in learning disabilities, and set out immediately to pursue a career in education. For ten years she held the position of demonstration teacher of young language-delayed children, while at the same time serving as a consultant to the California State Education Department. As a consultant she was responsible for assisting in determining policy affecting placement of children with learning disabilities. She also conducted workshops for parents and teachers.

At present Linda is in New York working for the New York City Board of Education as an educational consultant. She is involved in a number of training activities, among them developing a program to teach children who are diagnosed as autistic. She is also serving as an adjunct on a college faculty and is the chief architect of a course on how to teach autistic children.

What are Linda's future goals? To this question, Linda states what is already obvious—to work within the educational system in order to effect positive change for those persons who have disabilities.

9

STEPPING STONES

Things don't change but by and by our wishes change.

Proust

When is a job a stopping place along the highway of your career? When is it wiser to remain at your place of work? When would it be to your advantage to change fields? What do you do if your company folds beneath you, retrenches, or the entire industry threatens to dry up? How do you decide whether it's best to relocate with your company or take your chances at finding another job on at least an equal level with the one you now have? How can you effectively plan ahead?

As complex as getting your first job may be, the next step up the career ladder, especially when it involves a major career change, may tax all your ingenuity, prescience and skill. Of the possibilities, it is hardest to make a career change into a different field, for you are forfeiting saleable experience for an unknown, a fact that may nag at a prospective employer. The next possibility is making a career change in the same field, but with a different organization. If your particular skill is not in great demand, you will probably find that you are competing with a number of other qualified candidates for the same job. The third possibility is movement up the ladder within your own company or organization. Neither you nor the situation within the company holds any mystery. Your employer knows what you can do. You know what the opportunities for advancement are. All you need to do is work toward your promotion. Before you examine the three possibilities above, you need to look more closely at your motivation for change. Are you making the most of what you have or do you really need to change? Are you actually in a dead-end job or is it your approach and attitude that blind you to opportunities within the organization?

Come to Grips with Your Gripes

You desire change. You wish for something better, more dynamic, more consistent with your talents and capabilities, yet the fact that in order to get that other job you will need to leave the one in hand is often an effective restraint to change. In our experience at the agency, we interview many men and women who say they need a change of job—immediately, it would seem from the desperate look in their eyes, the litany of complaints against their present employer and the fears they so vividly express of being "stuck in a rut." We have learned over the years, however, that desire alone does not make a change. There is little doubt that each person sincerely wants to change to another job when in counsel with us, but the time may not be ripe for the break from the old into the new. What one day appears to be an intolerable situation, the next day becomes operable. What seems to be a quantity of jobs out there becomes, upon closer examination, jobs requiring specific qualifications. What in dreams seems to be an easy transitional process becomes in reality a repetition of the frustrations and disappointments inherent in the job hunt.

It is important, therefore, to examine your reasons for wanting to change jobs. Weigh what you have achieved in seniority; compare the benefits of your pension plan and fringe benefits with what other companies are offering and balance what you already know about a company's operation with the unknowns of a new organization. Some of the situations driving you to want to change may include:

1. *Lack of promotion:* "I'm as good as the next fellow who was hired about the same time. He/she's already

been promoted, and I'm still working in the typing pool (selling, digging ditches, etc.)''.

Six months after Tony was placed in his position, he again visited our office, complaining that he had been overlooked. When he was hired, he was promised that he would be first in line to move from trainee to assistant. We had also understood that Tony would be promoted rapidly. We called the personnel manager of the company who informed us that although Tony's work was commendable, his attendance was spotty, and as a result of his "no-shows," morale in the office was slipping. Solution: Tony rearranged his life so that he could be at work regularly and on time. He was promptly promoted and learned the lesson that talent alone does not an employee make. The other qualities of positive interaction with colleagues, willingness, flexibility, punctuality all contributed to success on the job. The first step, then, in examining why you may not be promoted is to consider your own contribution to the overall functioning of the organization.

The second step is to talk as frankly as possible to your employer. Discuss your needs and aspirations calmly. He or she can often predict if there will be an opportunity for promotion. If, indeed, no opportunity exists, then you have no choice. However, when conducted nonjudgmentally, these conversations can often open new directions for you within the company.

2. *I hate my boss:* "I can't stand working for that S.O.B. one more day. He/she rides me every minute, criticizes everything I do, makes me feel like two cents. I've got to get out."

    Why? Does everybody in your organization clash with your boss or are only you singled out? Is your boss the owner of the company? If you are made the scapegoat, attempt to analyze if indeed the problem may lie in your interpretation of your role. Is it possible you consciously or unconsciously provoke and antagonize him or her? Do your colleagues find the boss difficult? If everyone finds the boss difficult and he or she is the owner of the company, you have no choice but to leave when the situation becomes untenable. However, if the person who supervises you is difficult, then you and your colleagues might let management know that work in your department suffers as a result of your supervisor's attitude. If there is no way to work from within to diffuse the animosity that exists you may find that your best move is onward and outward.

3. *I'm in a dead-end job:* "When I took this job I was told there would be no place to go, but I needed the work. Now I see it's really true. I've got to move on or I'll lose my sanity."

    See *lack of promotion.* Keep in mind that many small, seemingly unpromising situations have been turned to an individual's advantage as a result of his or her ideas and vision.

4. *Travel time—getting to work:* "It takes me too long to get to work. I'm traveling three to four hours each day. I never see my family. I need a job closer to home. It's too difficult for me to reach my job under present circumstances. I can't depend upon public transportation, and private transportation is too costly."

    Problems of travel can be one of the most legitimate reasons for seeking a job change. Commuting causes a certain amount of stress on the body which, added to the stress of working, can seriously impair your health. If your travel time is affecting both your efficiency on the job and your social and family life, a change is certainly recommended. You may be faced also with the problems of public transportation. Although there is great pressure to provide a paratransit network for the disabled, movement in this direction has been sluggish. Seeking a job change whereby traveling to and from the job will be less of a problem may actually be the wisest move for you.

5. *Working conditions:* "If you worked where I work, you'd throw up. The conditions are terrible. No air-conditioning in summer; inadequate heat in the winter. The janitor doesn't even keep the place clean."

Working conditions can often be improved, provided you have a group of employees who are interested in seeking to make change. Often, when you work for a union shop, working conditions become part of the labor negotiations. Rather than stewing about the state of affairs, make a few suggestions to your boss or supervisor about the conditions. The press of business may blind your superiors to their employee's comforts and needs. A word to the wise may be sufficient to change conditions. If, however, when after you have taken action, working conditions do not improve and may indeed be injurious to your health, then you should certainly seek change. There is no need to suffer physically on the job.

6. *Health:* "I can't work in that place and be exposed to dangerous chemicals. I'm endangering myself and my unborn children. Get me out!"

As our technology becomes more complex, the effluents of our society present greater and greater environmental problems. Workers are often torn between the desire to earn a good salary and the dangers of working with toxic materials. Change is certainly indicated if your work place is dangerous to your health, and if the company is not taking the necessary precautions to protect you.

7. *Too much overtime!* "If I spend another Saturday or evening on the job, I'll scream. I don't have a life of my own."

Workaholics welcome this kind of job. If you are unfortunate enough to find yourself in a den of workaholics and feel guilty clocking out at five, then this job is not for you. There are times when the nonworkaholic survives nicely with more hard-driving peers, but the pressure of work in an organization of this kind often spills over to everybody involved, and those who do not put in their share of overtime are resented.

8. *Too much pressure:* "I can't stand it. My nerves are raw from the pressure. No sooner do I begin one thing than there's another crisis. I'm not fit to live with when I come home. And I think I'm getting high blood pressure."

Depending upon your constitution, pressure can add to the excitement of your career or can be the cause for emotional and physical problems. Analyze what pressure is doing to you. Have you tried a job without pressure? If so, were you bored? Is the pressure caused by the job or by your own need for perfection? We recently talked to Jane, who complained that the pressure on the job was so intense that she was going home with a headache every day. Since we had placed other people with the same company and had not heard this complaint before, we questioned Jane closely about her work habits. As we talked together, a pattern of self-induced pressure emerged, and Jane began to realize her contribution to pressure. On the other hand, a job may truly be a boilermaker. If you are unconstitutionally unable to handle this kind of job, then by all means make a move where the action is less intense.

9. *Too little to do:* "I like my job well enough, but I don't have enough to do. I have to look busy all the time because I'm in the front office, but I'm fast and turn the work out in no time at all."

At the other end of the pressure pole is the job that drags. You're paid reasonably well, you arrive on time, leave on time, but you yawn yourself through the day. Analyze your position carefully if you're in this kind of job. Does your supervisor know you're a speed demon? Are there other kinds of work you can take on, thus saving the organization money and possibly promoting yourself to a more responsible position? Often, we find, top echelon is so busy flying around trying to take care of a myriad of detail that they are unaware of some of the problems that exist in the office. The more helpful you become on the job, the more valuable you will be to your employer. However, you may indeed be working with an organization where there is a minimum of activity. If you're the kind of person who enjoys being busy, feel productive only when you're fully engaged in work, fear going stale if you're not working to capacity, then, indeed, you will need to find a job more suited to your temperament.

10. *No rapport with staff:* "I really can't stand the people I work with. They're nice enough, but they don't think the way I do. Their political or religious beliefs are so different that I feel like an outsider. They don't understand the nature of my disability."

It often happens. You're different. You feel different. You are different. You expect the staff to understand your differences and accept them. You're accustomed to differences, of course, but now that you're in the working world and competing with everybody else, doing the same kind of work, you can't understand some of the attitudes you encounter. You are your own spokesperson here. Even though the general public has been exposed to theatre, film, documentaries, literature and in many cases personal experience with persons who have handicapping conditions, they may still be awkward in their treatment of you. They may not know whether to ignore your disability or to discuss it with you, to protect you or let you fend for yourself. You may find that you need to educate your colleagues to what it is you can and cannot do, and that although differences exist, they fade when similarities are compared.

When the problem is not one of ignorance about the handicapping condition but rather a lack of common interests, you may experience minor or major discomforts in associating with your colleagues. If the discomfort becomes acute and you no longer enjoy working for the organization, then perhaps you should look for the kind of work that attracts people like yourself.

11. *Salary:* "I'm not being paid enough. I can't live on what I make. I've got to moonlight to make ends meet and that's pretty difficult for me."

Nobody ever feels he or she is being paid enough. Every time you get a raise, inflation pinches it back as deftly as you would pinch back a chrysanthemum bush. If you do feel that you're being underpaid, take a personal survey of similar jobs in your area. Compare your salary, fringe benefits, time of travel and convenience with other jobs where the salary might be greater but the fringes less and travel more extensive. Weigh all the factors before you leap. If you decide that you can only raise your standard by seeking a job at a higher salary, begin your search. In this case, we strongly urge that you seek a job while still employed. The money lost between the time you leave your present job and locate your next job may be considerable.

12. *Grass is greener elsewhere:* "There must be a better job somewhere else. My friend, my friend's friend, my aunt, my uncle, my niece, my nephew (choose one or add some of your own) have absolutely great jobs."

Always. It's human nature. Joe, John or Mary will tell you about the work they're doing. You'll read about the remarkable success of someone just like yourself. You'll hear a story about a person who made it with less skills and education than you have. There is no reason you can't move on to another job if you feel you can do better, but please, examine each new possibility carefully to see if you're not making a change merely for the sake of change, and in the process giving up a job that serves you well.

Admittedly, the list we have compiled is short compared to the many reasons that may provoke you to consider change.

However, judging from our experiences with persons who want to change jobs, some time spent in sober reflection is valuable before stepping to the next stone.

Career or Job—Evaluate Your Present Employment

When you have thoroughly analyzed your attitude and explored in depth your reasons for wanting to change, you should carefully consider possibility number three: advancement within your own organization. If you are working for city, county, state or federal government, promotion from within is primarily through examination to higher level positions. To prepare for these examinations, you may need to take additional courses and/or become certified in a particular field. Each step along the way is spelled out, and since affirmative action applies to promotion as well as hiring practices, you are entitled to take these examinations with the necessary modifications.

The general marketplace requires a somewhat different approach. Your competence is not measured by your scores on an examination, but your actual job performance. Since you are at the "stepping stone" stage, you have probably entered your present job as a trainee, and may now be working at one or two steps beyond the trainee level. Promotion depends to a large extent on your job performance at this level. Those who get ahead are those who put out. They're not clock watchers. They understand priorities. They don't allow their personal lives to interfere with the job. They like responsibility. They're interested in the management point of view as well as that of the workers. They indicate in many ways that they are in agreement with company policy, and if not in agreement, are willing to work out compromises that will be amenable to both management and the worker.

Interestingly, although there are no examinations to score you into a more responsible position, the business community is well aware of the importance of upgrading skills. You may find that courses taken at colleges and universities may provide the lever for a more responsible position.

On the other hand, you may decide that the work you are doing will not lead to a better position within the company. Or you may be bored with the work you are presently doing, or you may simply resent the amount of overtime necessary to get the job done. Shirley B. decided to become an accountant even though she was a successful production manager on a trade newspaper. When her firm found that she had accounting credentials, they promptly offered her a transfer to the accounting department, pleased at retaining a loyal worker. Shirley traded an ulcer-producing, time-consuming job for a steady-paced job with regular hours. Both Shirley and her company are pleased with the transition.

Possibilities one and two can be grouped together. It is more difficult to make a career change into a different field. Nevertheless, with additional training, this change can be accomplished. The important message here is that when you want to move out, when you have finally made the decision to change, then by all means go to it. Change, as we indicated previously, is at times the most difficult thing to do. Career specialists have found that the average person changes jobs four times in his or her working life, and about half of these people actually change fields.

Check your job sources (chapter 5) if you are still working. Be discreet. Analyze the market. What kind of job do you feel you are now best equipped to handle? Ubiquitous phrases such as "something with growth potential," "something creative," "something challenging," "something where I can use what I'm really interested in," tend to obfuscate rather than clarify what it is you want to do. One of the best sources for job titles and capsule descriptions is the classified section of your newspaper. Another source is the classified section of journals and periodicals relating to your particular field. These sources will tell the kinds of jobs that are on the market. You will see that your search for your second, third or fourth job is actually not that much different from your search for your first job. You merely use your sources more knowledgeably and judiciously. You plan a job campaign. You inform people who know of your work that you are in the market. What makes this search different from your initial endeavor is that you now have achieved a background of experience, met a good number of people who know of your work and, having been through the process once, can organize your campaign effectively.

When you decide to change, hang in there until you have located a new job. Employers tend to hire people who are presently working. Employed, your chances are greater that you will receive more job offers. Another reason for staying on the job is to minimize the stress of finding a new one. It's more comfortable to look for a job when you already have one. Don't be seduced by the fact that the job you want may seem to exist for only a short time. Companies may not recruit for several months, but a change in the economic situation will send them scouting for prospective employees. Employment agencies whose existence depends on the continuance of job openings remain in business whether the economy is bullish or bearish. The job market is in constant flux; people retire, others move, departments expand, companies relocate, new regions open up, new industries emerge. Whenever there is fear that an industry is drying up, it appears that technology produces another to take its place. Witness the burgeoning computer industry.

Finding the job that will give you that step to the higher position may, therefore, take time. It is not unusual for a person who is job hunting to look for six months to a year before finding a suitable position. If you are still working, hold out for a job that matches your needs and aspirations.

Deliberate Stepping Stones

There are a number of jobs that may or may not lead to better opportunities, but are worth investigating for both the experience gained and the access into an organization.

Temporary Jobs

The temporary job often serves as an excellent stepping stone. You have the opportunity of working with a number of companies on a temporary basis. Your ability to get a job done quickly, efficiently and effectively is not lost to those in charge. More often than not, our temporary counselors are asked to refer a particularly good temporary worker for a permanent position. Both private employment agencies and the placement divisions of vocational rehabilitation agencies cite temporary employment as an ideal way of gaining entree into the job market. One counselor told us about Eleanor, a whiz of a typist who incidentally had a hearing impairment. She was placed temporarily in the typing pool. Each member of the pool, however, was required to spend two hours a day on the switchboard. Eleanor offered to type up another employee's work if she would take double time at the switchboard. The arrangement worked so well that Eleanor was hired permanently. The other members of the typing pool welcomed the extra break from typing afforded them as a result of the exchange of duties with Eleanor. What began as accommodation became accepted practice.

Part-Time Work

A part-time job fulfills much the same function as temporary work but is usually permanent. Persons returning to work after having completed a vocational training or rehabilitation program often find that part-time work is more suitable than the forty-hour week. Traditionally, part-time work meets the needs of young mothers with school-age children who want to be at home when their children return from school. But other persons whose energy is limited may find part-time the most appropriate means of work activity. Part-timers often find themselves faced with a dilemma. As their efficiency and responsibility grow, the workload increases. The result—you the part-timer are offered a full-time position with greater responsibility and a sizeable increase in salary.

Job Sharing

Another form of part-time work might be sharing one full-time job. You work at the job in the morning. In the afternoon, your partner picks up where you left off. Thus, a full-time job is completely covered by two responsible people. Job sharing, as with part-time, can lead to more permanent work if you decide that you are ready to work full time.

Funded Jobs

If you have a particular skill, you might want to investigate a number of one- two- or three-year jobs funded through federal and state grants. Most often, these jobs are found in nonprofit agencies or educational institutions, but at times companies have set aside funds or are participating in a government project in which they are demonstrating a work incentive plan for a particular segment of the population. Naturally, these jobs do not offer longevity but they are usually exciting, involving and stimulating. The experience gained is transferable to any number of permanent positions. As stepping stones, they offer the opportunity for you to prove your mettle. If you are the project director, you will be establishing a reputation in the field. If you are interested in funded jobs, you will need to use a little ingenuity to unearth them. Try your schools, colleges and universities, social service agencies, neighborhood action groups, Mayor's Office of the Handicapped, Governor's Committee on the Handicapped, personnel departments of large organizations, libraries, friends and acquaintances working in the field.

A Few Pointers

- A temporary job can be a stepping stone. A part-time job can be a stepping stone. A short-term job (lasting one, two, three years) can be a stepping stone.

- When ready to move onto a new job, examine your present situation; examine your attitudes on your present job; examine the potential within your own organization; examine if you need more courses or training; explore the job market; and decide what you want to do in advance.

- Plan your job campaign by developing a good resume; looking into all job sources; using systematic job hunting techniques; and getting in touch with people who can help you, both privately and professionally.

PART III

ALTERNATIVES

10

ADDITIONAL TRAINING

Part of the pleasure of living in a free society is found in the numerous opportunities for choice. You can choose what you want to wear, where you want to eat, live or go to school. There is freedom of movement implicit in everything you do. Nevertheless, if you examine each choice carefully, you will find that freedom is tempered by ability. Should you want to live in a specific section of the country, you will first need to know that you will be able to earn a living there and find a home within your price range. Whatever it is you choose to do, you must have the wherewithal to do it.

The job market is no exception. Your choice of job depends often on the preparation you have made for assuming that job. Wishing for skills or hoping that the prospective employer will divine a spark of creativity based solely on your own estimation of what you can do—while it may be an accurate assessment— is considered by the majority of employers as sheer fantasy. A talent for art can be considerably strengthened with appropriate courses, an aptitude for languages can be fully realized through learning several of them, an ability with figures can escalate you into a controller's job if you get the proper credentials.

Whatever the job, the bridge between you and your future employer is production. Can you do the job? Will you do the job better than the other people who have been interviewed? Are you the best person for the job? Production knows no boundaries. It is as relevant in the business world as on a college campus. It may appear in different guises, but it remains the cornerstone for hiring, retaining and promoting.

Preparation and production are in some ways synonymous. The more you know, the more you can do; the better educated or trained you are, the greater your value to your employer. We do not mean to imply that you should immediately apply for matriculation in a Ph.D. program. By no means. In our society there is often too great a stress on formal education and too little emphasis on job readiness. Our primary thrust in this chapter, therefore, is to help you explore the many and varied opportunities available to you for further study and preparedness. In some cases you will find that you never need to leave your home; in others you can be trained directly on the job. If you prefer the college route, you will find that colleges and universities are, for the most part, complying with regulations governing access for handicapped persons.

Vocational Rehabilitation Programs

Before setting off on your own, you might want to investigate the resources of the State Office of Vocational Rehabilitation. This comprehensive vocational rehabilitation program is a joint effort of federal and state governments. It is designed to assist physically or mentally handicapped individuals to take advantage of special education and training in order to prepare them for jobs. Services without charge and regardless of income include:

- an evaluation of your rehabilitation potential

- counseling, guidance and referral services

- placement and postemployment follow-up

Eligibility for the program covers a wide spectrum. You may apply if your disability interferes with continued employment or employability, or disrupts your ability to function. All disabilities are considered including those that are severely handicapping. Levels of employment depend upon the nature of your handicapping condition.

You are entitled to services of evaluation, counseling and placement without cost. However, you may be required to contribute to other services such as medical, therapeutic and training or related services, as determined by financial need.

The process through which the State Office of Vocational Rehabilitation agency prepares you for a job involves the development of an individualized written rehabilitation program (IWRP). You and your counselor agree to long-range and short-term rehabilitative and employment goals. You need to have an aim in mind when you sit down with your counselor. Are the skills you will feel most comfortable in learning compatible with the job market? Will you receive adequate training so that you will be able to do the job efficiently? Will the agency assist you in the settling-in period? Will the agency find you a job?

Your counselor is prepared to assist you in obtaining whatever education or training is commensurate with your ability. At times, college admission may pose a problem due to depressed SAT scores. Linda S., because of inadequate programming in her special education classes at high school, found that she did not pass the SAT with high enough scores for college admittance. On the strength of these scores, Linda's counselor tried to dissuade her from pursuing a college education, but Linda, undaunted, investigated colleges on her own and found one that would accept her scores provided she maintained a B average for the first two semesters. Linda did better than a B. She made the Dean's list.

Many private organizations primarily involved with the handicapped offer special training programs. TAPS of the Epilepsy Foundation, the National Association of Retarded Citizens (with its on-the-job training programs operating in forty-eight states), the Federation of Jewish Philanthropies (of which the Jewish

Vocational Services throughout the nation and the exemplary Federation of Employment and Guidance Services in New York are members), the Commission for the Blind, ICD Rehabilitation and Research Center are just a few of the organizations committed to helping disabled citizens find their working place in society. (See Appendix III, IX for a more comprehensive listing.)

Sources for education and training are thus available to you from a variety of agencies, both public and private. Information on funding can be obtained through your high school, your state vocational counselor, your state employment counselor or your financial aid officer at a college of your choice.

Colleges and Universities

You cannot depend upon one or two sources to provide access to all the alternatives available to you. You may find that your own research can help you and your counselor plan the best course of action for you. Therefore, it is a good idea to examine the many opportunities for postsecondary education. Since the passage of Section 504 of the Rehabilitation Act of 1973, qualified individuals may not be denied admission to colleges or universities. This act applies to those community, state and private colleges and universities and postsecondary vocational education programs that receive governmental funds. Since just about every institution in the United States receives funds from the federal government, the prospect that you can attend the college of choice, provided you meet the academic requirements, is good.

According to Section 504, the institution receiving federal funds must be prepared to make specific adaptations to meet your need. Since 1980 was the deadline for compliance, you should find a number of programs and activities to be accessible. Accessibility can be defined in terms of your being able to take any class you wish within the institution. The law explicitly states that full accessibility must encompass a full range for persons with handicapping conditions. These services include providing access or modifying the environment for persons who are physically impaired in locomotion or confined to wheelchairs, have coordination difficulties, visual handicaps, hearing handicaps, speech and language impairments, learning disabilities, and mental and psychological disorders. When an institution plans programs for persons with disabilities, the planning team must have as part of its membership a person or persons who are disabled.

Consistent with the philosophy of mainstreaming, institutions cannot separate you from regular classes. Nor can you be excluded from academic, research or occupational training programs solely on the basis of your handicap.

Whatever programs are offered to the nondisabled must also be offered to you. These comparable programs may include: accessible housing, financial assistance, personal, academic or vocational counseling guidance, placement service, physical education, athletics and extracurricular activities, health programs, insurance plans, transportation and recreation.

The law further requires that full participation cannot be categorical by handicap. For example, you may or may not want to take advantage of readers in the library if you have a visual impairment, or use interpreters if you have a hearing disability, but the services must exist should you desire to use them. If these services do not exist, there should be a channel through which you can redress grievances.

Catalogues, student handbooks, brochures, written materials regarding financial assistance and other literature for prospective students should contain that institution's commitment to nondiscriminatory practices.

Flexibility is the keyword. It is important when you enter an institution of your choice that you and your adviser work out a feasible plan for your course study. You may find that you will need more time to complete the degree requirements. Or you may want to substitute one course for another. For example, if you have a hearing loss, you might take a course in art history rather than music appreciation; if visually limited the reverse might be better for you. You will need to ascertain what auxiliary aids are available to help you keep up with the educational demands. Are there taped or brailled texts in the library? Is there access to interpreters? Can equipment be adapted to meet your needs if you are physically impaired? Is there a special program for you if you have a learning disability? As stated previously, these adjustments must be made if an institution is to comply with the spirit and letter of the law.

Section 504 extends its protective arm to admission requirements as well. Testing for postsecondary schools must be fair. This means that college admission tests take into account sensory, manual or speech impairments. You can expect: test editions in braille, large type, extended time, readers, separate test rooms and other kinds of assistance, depending upon your need. For more information on adapted college admission programs, write to: Admission Testing Program for Handicapped Students (ATP), College Entrance Examinations Board, Box 592, Princeton, New Jersey 08540.

Financial Aid

All financial aid is open to you. Financial aid packages change constantly, so it is best to consult with your financial aid officer of the college or university of your choice for the latest information.

It is also a good idea to investigate whether there are specific scholarship funds available for the handicapped. Your high school guidance counselor, your vocational counselor and your financial aid officer at college will be able to help you in this regard. A guide that can be found in your public library, *A Chance to Go to College: A Directory of 800 Colleges that Have Special Help for Students from Minorities and Low Income Families,* published by the College Entrance Examination Board, 888

Seventh Avenue, New York, New York 10019, is a good source of information.

Accessibility

You can obtain information about an individual campus by writing to the Governor's Committee on Employment of the Handicapped (see Appendix VII for addresses) or you can check directly with the college of your choice. A complete directory of colleges developed from a survey conducted by the President's Committee on Employment of the Handicapped can be obtained from ABT Associates, Inc., 55 Wheeler Street, Cambridge, Massachusetts 02138. The price is $12 for handicapped students and their families; $18.50 for libraries, schools and other institutions.

Free of charge from the President's Committee on Employment of the Handicapped, Washington, D.C. 20210, is *Getting Through College With a Disability: A Summary of Services Available on 500 Campuses for Students with Handicapping Conditions.*

Bear in mind, however, that changes are occurring daily at institutions. Whatever publication you use, take the extra time to corroborate the information through a direct letter, phone call or visit to the college of your choice.

Other directories that might be useful are:

- *A Guide to College/Career Programs for Deaf Students,* Office of Demographic Studies, Gallaudet College, Kendall Green, Washington, D.C. 20002.

- *A National Directory of Four Year Colleges, Two Year Colleges and Post High School Training Programs for Young People with Learning Disabilities,* Partners in Publishing, Box 50347, Tulsa, Oklahoma 74150.

- *Handbook for Blind College Students,* National Federation of the Blind, 218 Randolph Hotel Building, Des Moines, Iowa 50309.

- *The College Guide for Students with Disabilities,* ABT Publications, 55 Wheeler Street, Cambridge, Massachusetts 02138.

Alternative College Programs

The stereotype of entering college and graduating with an A.S. or B.S. degree within a two- to four-year period has fortunately given way to a proliferation of programs designed to meet individual needs. Some of these programs range from College Level Examination Program (CLEP), external degree programs such as New York Regents External Degree Program (RED), and Board for State Academic Awards (BSAA), Credit for Life Experience, TV College, Weekend College to correspondence schools, homebound programs, and degrees by examination. In some cases, a high school diploma may be bypassed in favor of demonstration that an individual can handle college material. Often programs are developed with the help of advisers associated with the program. There may be a combination of correspondence courses and courses taken on campus, or in the case of the homebound, all courses will be through correspondence. The programs that we will be describing in this section are only a small sampling of those available to you. If you are choosing a program without the help of a vocational counselor, move cautiously. Be sure that the courses you take are accredited.

College By Examination (CLEP)

A CLEP examination consists of two types of tests that measure knowledge regardless of how it is acquired. Five broad areas—English composition, humanities, social science/history, mathematics and natural science—are further broken down into a series of multiple choice tests measuring ability in a variety of subjects. Special arrangements are made to test handicapped persons. Four out of five general examinations (humanities is the exception) have been put on cassette tapes for administration to blind persons. Handicapped individuals may be tested separately if they wish, and may request twice the normal amount of time. Readers may also be appointed by handicapped candidates. If you plan to take a CLEP test, contact your nearest CLEP Center for information on adaptation for your particular disability, prior to registration (check Appendix XI for college board offices).

External Degree Programs

The CLEP program, although generally considered an opportunity for more advanced standing in a college or university, also offers the possibility of achieving a degree through the external degree programs. Currently four states, Connecticut, Illinois, New Jersey and New York, offer external degrees. With the exception of Illinois, which requires some time on campus, classroom attendance is not mandatory. These programs are open to out-of-state individuals as well as residents. The fees are usually higher for out-of-state residents. Persons completing the external degree programs may sit for state licensing examination. There appears to be general acceptance of these programs in graduate schools as well as in business, since the course of study is as rigorous as can be found on a college campus.

Proficiency Examination Program (PEP); American College Testing Program (ACT)

While the CLEP programs measure knowledge gained regardless of how it was acquired, the PEP programs operate through the American College Testing Program. In New York, for example, ACT, in connection with the New York Regents External Degree Program (RED), is used to assess knowledge for credits specifically in the RED program. Therefore, the ACT-PEP tests are divided into two series: The College Proficiency Examination Program (CPEP) and the Regents External Degree Examination. For more information, write to ACT/PEP, 1 Dupont Circle, N.W., Washington, D.C. 20036; ACT/PEP, P.O. Box 168, Iowa City, Iowa, and College Proficiency Examination Program, State

Department of Education, Empire State Plaza, Albany, New York 12230.

Should you be interested in the RED program, you can obtain phone numbers of advisers by writing to Linda Headly Walker, Coordinator of Volunteer Advisor Network, Regents External Degrees, College Proficiency Examination Program, The University of the State of New York, Cultural Education Center, Room 5D45, Albany, New York 12230.

Other external degree programs such as the Empire State College, State University of New York, the Board for State Academic Awards (BSAA) in Connecticut, and the University of Mid-America with affiliations with the University of Iowa, Iowa State University, the University of Kansas, Kansas State University, the University of Nebraska, the University of Minnesota, the University of Missouri, the University of North Dakota, North Dakota State University, the University of South Dakota and South Dakota State University, similarly offer independent adult learners the opportunity to earn an academic degree through a variety of alternative approaches. These programs are sensitive to the needs of adult learners and offer a variety of settings and arrangements. For example, the Empire State College works on a contract system with its students. A contract may involve independent study, a correspondence course, a course designed for independent study, or a formal course on the campus of another college of the SUNY system. The program is highly individualized and designed to meet each student's personal needs. Out-of-state students are welcome. Write to the Empire State College, 2 Union Avenue, Saratoga Springs, New York 12866 for more information. A similar program exists within the BSAA. Write to the Board for State Academic Awards, 340 Capitol Avenue, Hartford, Connecticut 06115. The University of Mid-America utilizes both traditional and nontraditional components, including video lessons for broadcast by educational television stations, popularized material for newspaper publication, and audiocassette tapes, study guides and textbooks for independent study at home. Write to the Division of Public Affairs, University of Mid-America, Terminal Building, 10th and O Streets, P.O. Box 82006, Lincoln, Nebraska 68501; phone number: 800-228-4572, or 402-474-2300.

TV Courses

The use of television to bring college-level instruction into your home is a steadily growing enterprise. Check your local college or university to see if a program exists in your area.

Credit for Nontraditional Courses

You may want to take advantage of the opportunity to have courses you've taken evaluated for college credit. These courses may have been delivered in nontraditional settings such as those given by private employers, community organizations, labor unions, governmental agencies. The American Council on Education, Office of Educational Credit, 1 Dupont Circle, N.W., Washington, D.C. 20036 publishes annually *A Guide to Educational Programs in Noncollegiate Organizations.*

Credit for Experience

Credit for experience can be evaluated through the Council for Advancement of Experiential Learning (CAEL), American City Building, Suite 212, Columbia, Maryland 21044. Some three hundred and fifty colleges and universities belonging to this organization give credit for experience. With the help of a counselor at any of the participating institutions, you can identify and document what you have learned through work and/or volunteer service. Along the same lines, the Council of National Organizations for Adult Education's Task Force on Volunteer Accreditation has developed a book entitled *I Can: A Tool for Assessing Skills Acquired Through Volunteer Experience.* This publication may be purchased from Ramco Associates, 228 East 45th Street, New York, New York 10017. In addition, the Educational Testing Service (ETS) has developed several lists for identifying and assessing volunteer and homemaker skills. Their publication, *How to Get Credit for What You Have Learned as a Homemaker or Volunteer,* may be purchased from ETS, Princeton, New Jersey 08540.

Weekend College

More and more colleges are incorporating the weekend concept into their curriculum offerings. Most of these courses follow a traditional course of study, but hours and locations are nontraditional. Check your local college or university if you are interested in gaining your degree through attending only on weekends.

Colleges with Learning Disability Programs

Typically a college that has a program for you if you have a learning disability offers a range of services and assistance. Programs emphasize the development of self-learning skills and are soundly grounded in educational philosophy. Admittance to these programs is usually based on better than average conceptual ability, sound emotional health, strong motivation for academic learning and diagnostic material identifying the learning disability. Following the precepts of Section 504, these programs are integrated with the general population, but in addition offer an array of services that may include counseling that takes the form of one-to-one; videotape and feedback; group sessions; tutoring to help you establish self-monitoring skills and develop organizational routines, learning to ask questions, help in taking notes; provision of tape recorders; access to resources such as financial aid, textbook sources (dyslexic students can qualify for textbooks for the blind). For a more comprehensive list of what each college program offers, check *A Guide to Post-Secondary Educational Opportunities for the Learning Disabled,* Time Out to Enjoy, Inc., 113 Garfield Street, Oak Park, Illinois 60304. The price of this book is $12.00, but it may be found in your local library. If you don't find a college in your vicinity listed in the book, call your local college and inquire if it has a special program for the learning-disabled. Since the writing of this guide, a number of other colleges have instituted programs.

Correspondence Courses/Home Study

Perhaps the most independent method of advanced study is through correspondence courses. As we have indicated previously, many of these courses will be acceptable to some of the alternative programs provided you have studied with an accredited school. Member institutions of the National University Extension Association (NUEA), Division for Independent Study, sponsor a wide variety of correspondence and independent study courses and programs. For more information write to National University Extension Association, 1 Dupont Circle, Washington, D.C. 21036. The National Home Study Council (NHSC), at 1601 18th Street, N.W., Washington, D.C. 20009, will send you a list of accredited correspondence schools along with materials about the council's objectives. They will tell you whether you can receive assistance in making decisions on a course of study, what credits you may expect for experience, and which credits you can take by examination. Currently there are six NHSCA accredited home study schools offering degree programs that may be earned entirely through correspondence study. NHSC will send you this updated list on request. You may also wish to send for the *NOCEA Guide to Independent Study Through Correspondence Instruction,* Peterson's Guides, Book Order Division, Box 978, Edison, New Jersey 08817.

Junior Colleges

Junior colleges are especially interested in opening their doors to you. Many of the colleges offer specialized programs geared to a particular handicap. One such program at New York University's School of Education, Health, Nursing and the Arts Professions trains young adults who learn more slowly, to become paraeducators. This two-year program has a success rate of about 70 percent job placement after graduation in education and other related situations. A similar program is conducted by Dr. Roberta Berns at Saddleback Community College, Mission

Viejo, California. This program trains handicapped students to become educational assistants.

Many private technical schools are listed as junior colleges and offer an A.A. (Associate in Arts) or an A.S. (Associate in Sciences) degree. They are equivalent to your first two years at a regular college, and for the most part are accepted if you wish to transfer to a four-year college, placing you in junior standing. Basically, however, the purpose of a junior college is to prepare you to enter the world of work at the technician or mid-management level. Courses range broadly over areas such as applied arts, business and commerce, ecology, health, medical and support services, home management, military science, repair services, public services, trade and technical services. Further information as to the extent of curriculum and location of junior colleges can be found in *Barron's Guide to Two-Year Colleges*.

The Nondegree Route

If the production of what we take for granted depended only on those persons who have earned college degrees, a great many services and goods would cease to exist. There are innumerable jobs requiring minimal training. These are jobs that are skill-oriented, acquired either on the job or through vocational and technical programs. Since the Vocational Rehabilitation Act of 1973 was passed, the number of opportunities for vocational training has escalated in both the public and private sectors. As we mentioned earlier in this chapter, both public and private institutions are engaged in setting up programs to train you for specific jobs in business and industry.

Private Nonprofit Vocational Training Programs

We have previously mentioned institutions prepared to assist you in finding or actually offering specialized training. It is important that you explore the resources within your community and make a list of those organizations that have training programs. Your counselor may not be familiar with all the training programs that exist. Often a program is funded on a three-year grant, and its activities may not yet have reached the state office. Visit several of these programs on your own to see if their particular emphasis on training meets with your needs.

Private Trade and Technical Schools

Private trade or technical schools that offer a course of study geared to a particular industry are a good source for training. These schools cannot discriminate against accepting handicapping students if they receive federal funds. This funding can come from a variety of sources such as the Veterans Administration and the State Office of Vocational Rehabilitation. It is important to consider only those trade schools that are accredited. Information on accreditation can be obtained through writing to the National Association of Trade and Technical Schools, 2021 L Street, N.W., Washington, D.C. 20036. In most cases, however, if you are in close touch with your counselor at the state office of vocational rehabilitation, an accredited school will be recommended to you.

Continuing Education

Your local high school may be a good source for specialized courses. Public schools offer vocational education and also courses to help you pass the General Education Development Program (GED) or high school equivalency program. Contact your local school system for information on courses and on testing procedures.

Other sources for continuing education include: YMCAs, YMHAs, unions, organizations, business and noncredit college courses. Many of these courses are offered at low or no cost and can lead to job training or may simply be an interesting activity where you can explore your particular talents.

Apprenticeship

Springing up all over the country, revitalizing industry and commerce, is the concept of apprenticeship. In the days of the guilds, apprenticeship was the accepted method for learning a trade. But with the increasing emphasis on formal education, apprenticeship unfortunately took a back seat, except for those industries where on-the-job training was a necessary qualification for journeyworker status. Since 1973, however, apprenticeship in a number of industries has been making small but steady inroads on the hard-core unemployed. And since every federal program includes a clause that applies to training the handicapped, you too are entitled to participate in these programs.

Basically, apprenticeship or, as it is now referred to, on-the-job training, consists of preparing you to work in skilled trades and crafts. It consists of on-the-job training under the supervision of experienced workers with or without related class instruction. When you have completed the prescribed number of hours of training in a registered apprenticeship program, you are awarded a certificate of completion. Depending upon the trade, the number of hours translated into years may vary, from one to six years. The bulk of apprenticeship programs falls within the range of three to four years.

Apprenticeship covers a wide variety of fields. Over seven hundred organizations are presently involved in these programs, and as new fields open and expand, the need for apprentices follow suit. In most cases, the sponsor is the company, a group of companies, a public agency or a union. Often employers and unions form joint apprenticeship committees to determine both industry needs and the kind of training required.

An example of such a liaison is the Private Industry Council, located throughout large cities and counties in the United States. The council meets the needs of labor shortages through on-the-job or vocational training of individuals sponsored by a coalition

of the chambers of commerce and industry, the Economic Development Council and the National Alliance of Business. Responding to the Title VII challenge, members of these groups
created a partnership between local business and government to
deal with the twin problems of high unemployment and skill
shortages. Begun in 1979, this program has made impressive inroads into training the unemployed and the handicapped for jobs
where there are labor shortages. Training ranges from computer
repair to welding to diamond cutting. As with all apprenticeship
jobs, training may include on-the-job experience, classroom or
vocational and technical training at an institute.

The beauty of apprenticeship work is that payment for work
begins immediately. Although initial wages may be no more than
minimum wage, apprentices soon begin to receive 40 to 50 percent of the journey worker's wage and, when nearing the end of
the program, almost the full wage.

Qualifications for apprenticeship jobs vary. However, all applicants must be at least sixteen years old and physically able to
perform the job. Depending upon the job, courses in science,
math, physics may be necessary as well as a high school diploma
or certificate. In some cases related work experience is accepted
in lieu of formal training. Since the majority of these companies
are doing business with the government, compliance with Section 504 on hiring practices decrees that you be considered for
apprenticeship programs.

An apprenticeship program may grow into a business venture.
In New York City, in the shadow of a luxury high-rise building,
a mini-mall plaza exists. It contains a complex of six shops and
businesses run and operated by mentally retarded workers. This
on-the-job training project is sponsored by Contemporary Guidance Services, which operate several training programs throughout New York City.

For further information on apprenticeship programs, see Appendix IV.

Funding Sources

There are five federal financial aid programs:

1. Pell Grant (Basic Educational Opportunity Grant). This grant is based on financial need and it does not have to be paid back.

2. Supplemental Educational Opportunity Grant. For undergraduates only. This grant also does not have to be paid back. (The Basic Grant differs from the Supplemental Grant in that the Basic Grant is an entitlement. The Supplemental Grant is drawn from money provided each year by the Department of Education. When the set amount of funds is dispersed, funding for that year ceases.)

3. College Work-Study. This program provides jobs for students who need financial aid and who must earn a part of their educational expenses.

4. National Direct Student Loan. A low-interest loan to help you pay for your education after high school.

5. Guaranteed Student Loan. A guaranteed student loan at low interest made to you by a bank, credit union or savings and loan association to help you pay for your education after high school. This loan is insured by the Federal Government.

Important: Changes are occurring in the loan programs. Check your financial aid officer or your counselor for the most recent legislative rulings.

PAUL SOTTNEK

When Paul Sottnek walks into a room one is immediately struck by his grace and self-assurance. He participates naturally and easily in the general conversation and addresses each speaker in turn, impressing one with his depth of understanding and his general knowledge.

Since the age of 19, when he was stricken with spinal meningitis, Paul has been severely visually handicapped. The aftermath of the illness had a devastating effect on his college work, for he had to learn compensatory skills to enable him to complete his studies. Nevertheless, he did graduate and went on to law school, only to find that his interests lay elsewhere. He switched to Adelphi, where he was graduated with an M.S. in history.

Upon graduation, Paul began his job search. Few organizations were interested. He took a civil service examination and ranked highest in the city (100 percent), but still no takers. His disability, which had not handicapped him from attaining an exemplary college education, now appeared to be a stumbling block for the majority of prospective employers. Entry-level jobs did not require college degrees. Management trainee and professional jobs dangled beyond his reach.

Finally, a personal friend offered Paul a job in a new mental health facility. Although the friend voiced doubts that Paul could manage the paperwork, he nevertheless felt that Paul deserved the opportunity. So successful was Paul in this field of work that he returned to school to earn his academic credentials in social work. Thereafter, with this experience behind him, he found it considerably easier to locate jobs. While visiting his sister in Atlanta, he took and passed a civil service exam. His excellent score along with his work history landed him a position as a field worker. But Paul Sottnek preferred to work in the Northeast and returned to New York City after several months. Unfortunately, it took ten months of job searching before he finally found work as a supervisor with a small nonprofit store-front agency. This job was terminated when the funding ran dry. However, with his accumulated experience, he was able to fit neatly into a position in the Office of the Mayor's Committee on the Handicapped.

Is Paul ambitious? You bet. When the opportunity presents itself, he will be off to another job offering him greater scope. Paul's movement in the job world has been erratic but steady. Now with the experience he has gained, coupled with his excellent education and buttressed by his large circle of friends and acquaintances, both in public and private life, Paul feels that his outlook for future employment is good.

The marketplace is not his total concern. He has turned his energies to political and community activities. Currently, he is contemplating running for the State Assembly. He is captain of his local Democratic club and serves on the Community Planning Board. He is also on the Advisory Board of Case Intake Management at a Welfare Center, is a member of the Bay Ridge Mental Health Association and belongs to the local precinct council.

Is it any wonder then that when Paul Sottnek walks into a room, one senses the strength and substance behind his easy cordial manner—that here's a man who is a *doer.*

GOING INTO
BUSINESS

Some of us venture into the world of business with a jug of lemonade, plastic cups, an upturned box, a crudely printed sign and pray for a heat wave. Granted we're still in short pants and we haven't seen many summers go by, but we're onto our first business enterprise at the age of six. Success might spur us into other activities such as selling used comic books and toys, surplus vegetables from the garden, helping Mom and Pop in the store—in fact any activity where we can exploit our budding talent.

On the other hand, we may never give the business side of life a second thought except for the purchase of goods until we reach our retirement years, when we yearn for something to do or when, struck by some misfortune, we need to find something to occupy us—as does Mrs. G., who conducts her business from a park bench, selling hand-made potholders. What began as therapy to coax movement back into her hands following a stroke has evolved into a tiny but productive business.

Going into business for you no doubt lies somewhere in between these two extremes. It touches on your need to be your own boss, to be in control, to manage your own affairs, to be the one to make all the money, to apply your acumen to get the right results, to have your talents serve you, to be free to do as you please, go where you please, make the rules. Sounds great, yes! It also implies that you are responsible for other people, your time is not your own, you will work far harder than you have ever worked before, you can gripe to no one, failure can mean financial loss or bankruptcy, you are constantly worrying about getting more customers and satisfying those customers, you are involved with getting quality materials, you have workers' problems consisting of absenteeism, illness, unions, you are enmeshed in government regulations and standards. In other words, depending upon the size of your business, you may be trading independence for one big headache. For some of you, there is no other way. For others, the thought of that much responsibility is frightening. Perhaps, then, the first step before contemplating a business venture is to examine your motives. The short questionnaire below is adapted from one developed by the Small Business Administration. It may give you some insights into whether you have the temperament and resources to succeed in business.

Test Yourself

Personal Qualities

1. My physical health is ____ excellent ____ good ____ fair ____ poor.

2. I solve problems ____ easily ____ fairly easily ____ with difficulty ____ poorly.

3. I get along with people ____ very well ____ well ____ badly.

4. I take matters into my own hands ____ often ____ some of the time ____ seldom ____ never.

5. I am self-confident ____ always ____ sometimes ____ seldom ____ never.

6. I work best ＿＿＿ when supervised ＿＿ with groups ＿＿ alone.

7. In an emergency ＿＿ I need support ＿＿ I am the leader.

8. I like to take risks ＿＿ almost always ＿＿ after careful consideration ＿＿ sometimes ＿＿ never.

9. I make decisions ＿＿ quickly ＿＿ moderately quickly ＿＿ slowly ＿＿ seldom ＿＿ only in consultation.

Motivation

		Yes	No
1.	I want to be my own boss.	＿＿	＿＿
2.	I can market my own skill or product better than anyone else.	＿＿	＿＿
3.	I can't find a job.	＿＿	＿＿
4.	I don't think anyone will accept me.	＿＿	＿＿
5.	I've been in other people's businesses for years and now I want to try my own.	＿＿	＿＿
6.	I come from a long line of business operators.	＿＿	＿＿
7.	I have to prove that I can do something.	＿＿	＿＿
8.	Being in business will make me feel like a person.	＿＿	＿＿

Why I Think I Can Succeed

1. I know how to get financial resources. ＿＿ ＿＿

2. My business experience has been ＿＿ limited ＿＿ varied.

3. I have experience in my chosen field amounting to ＿＿＿ a short time ＿＿＿ a great deal of time.

4. Holding a responsible job is ＿＿＿ new ＿＿＿ not new to me.

5. I expect to work ＿＿＿ long hours ＿＿＿ less that I do now ＿＿＿ to fit work into my life pattern.

6. Immediate profits are ＿＿＿ important ＿＿＿ unimportant.

7. My expectations are ＿＿＿ high ＿＿＿ realistic ＿＿＿ so-so.

8. I have had volunteer experience as a ＿＿＿ fund raiser ＿＿＿ administrative officer ＿＿＿ recruiter ＿＿＿ PTA president ＿＿＿ other ＿＿＿＿＿＿＿＿＿＿＿＿＿＿.

Setting Up

1. I expect to run my business at home to ＿＿＿ minimize expenses ＿＿＿ because my movement is limited ＿＿＿ building regulations permit it.

2. I expect to conduct my business in other people's homes, because it is a service business such as: ＿＿＿ catering ＿＿＿ caring for pets; a skills business ＿＿＿ upholstering ＿＿＿ cleaning ＿＿＿ other ＿＿＿＿＿.

3. I expect to set up business in a ＿＿＿ shop ＿＿＿ neighborhood street ＿＿＿ shopping center ＿＿＿ downtown ＿＿＿ other ＿＿＿＿＿＿＿＿＿＿＿＿＿＿＿＿.

4. I will run my business through direct mail advertising ＿＿＿.

5. I will run my business by advertising in specialized papers ＿＿＿.

6. I will conduct my business through door-to-door sales
    ——— .

7. Other ————————————————————————— .

   This questionnaire is designed primarily to help you think
through and consider the variety of factors involved in your quest
for your own business. There are no right or wrong answers.
Your responses only serve to direct you to evaluate your willingness to invest time, money and energy into the project. For
example, if in the "Personal Qualities" section, you checked off
more than five of the following to read: health is fair or poor,
solve problems with difficulty, never take matters into your own
hands, never feel self-confident, work best when supervised,
need support in an emergency, never take risks but instead make
decisions only in consultation, it would appear that you are not
a likely candidate for opening up your own business.

   Your motivation, however, for going into business may be
powerful enough to overcome some of the personality traits that
work against success in business. Your need to be your own
boss and prove you can do something well, together with dis-
couragement at finding a job, may be the impetus that proves
the exception to the rule. Nevertheless, forewarned is fore-
armed. In the section, "Why I Think I Can Succeed," note that
long hours, responsibility, immediate profits and financial resources are among the criteria to be considered. Success in your
own business depends, to a great extent, on your ability to tap
successfully all the resources available to you and to be able to
delay gratification.

   If you have decided that business is for you, then by all means
take advantage of the resources available to you. Small business
enterprise, like motherhood, is a sacred American dream. Even
at the writing of this book, as conservatism spreads across the
nation, a bill under the title of the Small Business Innovation
Research Act has been introduced into Congress. If passed, this
bill would require that one percent of the research and devel-

opment funds be designated for small business. In terms of federal grants, this sum could reach about $360 million a year.

Where to Go for Help

Small Business Administration

Although the Small Business Innovation Research Act bill is still a dream, the efforts of the Small Business Administration are a reality. Since 1953, the Small Business Administration, created by Congress, seeks to encourage, assist and protect the interests of small businesses throughout the nation. Over a hundred local offices are prepared to help you improve on your management skills, ensure that you receive your fair share of government purchases, contracts and subcontracts, including the sales of government property, and make or guarantee loans, provided you meet the qualifications. The Small Business Administration also publishes a wide variety of management, technical and marketing publications, many of which are free of charge.

Until recently special funds were set aside for minorities, the handicapped and women. Unfortunately, at the time of this writing, cutbacks in funding have affected this sector, and although funding is still available, it is no longer discretionary. Pressure on Congress may reverse the decision, and you may want to support congresspersons who are interested in this law.

The Small Business Administration enthusiastically endorses the concept of going into business and wants you to join the twelve million owners of small businesses throughout the United States. Basically, there are three categories of assistances: management assistance, financial assistance and procurement assistance, all of which are available through your local SBA office.

Management Assistance

Even though you may think that all you need is financial backing to put you on "go," according to SBA, who report from figures provided by Dun and Bradstreet, Inc., nearly 93 percent of business failures are due not to lack of financing, but to incompetence, lack of managerial experience. Since approximately a thousand businesses fail each day, this analysis seems to be on target.

To counteract failure due to mismanagement, SBA offers a diversified program that includes business management courses, conferences, workshops and clinics open to anybody who is considering starting a business or who is already in business and wishes to update his or her skills, enlarge operations or enter new fields.

Frequently these activities are cosponsored with local chambers of commerce, banks and other lending agencies, and universities and colleges. Speakers and lecturers are drawn from the business leadership community, the Service Corps of Retired Executives (SCORE) and the Active Corps of Executives (ACE) and SBA personnel. Fees are nominal. Information is available from your management assistance officer at your nearest SBA office.

A second facet of the management assistance program offers individual counseling with knowledgeable volunteers. Volunteers are drawn from SCORE and members of such national organizations as the Federation of Business and Professional Women, the National Association of Accountants, the Association of Minority Certified Accountants, the Association of Industrial Engineers and others. These volunteers, who have expressed a desire to share their experience with you, are on call to assist you with problems that may arise.

A third management aid is through student and faculty counseling. If your business is floundering, your SBA office may be involved in a program with a nearby university, where part of the curriculum consists of working out solutions for actual business problems.

A fourth service, entitled Contracts Counseling, is mainly for existing businesses with specific problems requiring uncommon or specialized qualifications. This program operates under the jurisdiction of the SBA's Minority Enterprise Division and provides specialized consulting service. When you visit your local SBA office, check to see if your business problems fall into this category.

Financial Assistance

A problem that small businesses often face is establishing sufficient credit on which to borrow money. SBA may provide assistance to you through a variety of loan programs that guarantee up to 90 percent of loans through commercial lending institutions. When applying for a loan, you must show proof of having been turned down by a commercial bank or other commercial lender (two in a city over 200,000) before applying to SBA. Direct loans from SBA are the most difficult to obtain since SBA's supply of loan money is limited. The majority of loans are, therefore, made through banks or other commercial lenders. Unfortunately, at this writing, money previously set aside for handicapped assistance loans is no longer available.

Applying for a loan is something of an art. It can well make the difference between loan approval and refusal. The management assistance workshops are geared to provide information on loan application and are well worth investigating. You might want to take advantage also of private counseling with a SCORE or ACE volunteer. SBA cautions that preparation is the key. Thorough preplanning ensures greater chance for loan approval.

Procurement Assistance

You finally open your doors and institute your campaign for business contracts. An excellent source is the federal government. SBA can help you get your fair share of the goods and services the government purchases each year from private companies. If you think you have a product that the federal government is purchasing, make an appointment to see an SBA procurement officer. This specialist is prepared to assist you in the development of bids for those contracts and subcontracts awarded by the government. You will also be told of the kinds of products and services currently needed and given help in getting your name on the bidders' lists. You might be able to make use of the Procurement Automated Source System (PASS), another SBA program designed to respond to the requests of government agencies and major corporations by profiling potential bidders who have merchandise or services to sell. Be sure to ask for more information when you talk to your procurement assistance officer.

Choose a Business

With the federal government behind you, all you need to do is review your talents and financial assets and set up your business. In these days of conglomerates and multinationals, it is remarkable that so many small businesses continue to exist and thrive. Yet throughout the world, the ingenuity, determination and acumen of the individual to found and maintain a business keeps alive a most important segment of our society.

Your business may start out as a cottage industry (working from your home), as Betty's does. She discovered that her husband's profession of optometry provided the exact challenge for her. She's busy escalating a direct-mail-order business involving the wholesaling of frames to optometrists and opticians. At present she's working from home, but she can foresee that she will be opening an office soon. The fact that she's in a wheelchair doesn't stop her one bit. In fact, Betty says, it helps her to organize what she needs to do more efficiently.

The love of a sport or an activity such as camping can oftentimes lead to a business. Albert, who lost an arm in World War II found, with his wife Fay that the only way they could vacation with their growing family was through taking camping trips. They enjoyed the experience so much that they decided to purchase a few trailers and rent them out so that their friends and acquaintances could share the experience. With the proceeds, they bought a few more trailers, and turned to sales rather than rentals. Today, they have a million-dollar business with branches in two states.

An idea whose time has come often spurs a new business. Janet, an advertising copywriter, was enchanted with the quality of her aunt's simulated diamond earrings. She suspected a large untapped market existed for these jewels. She contacted the manufacturer, who was only too pleased to sell her the jewels wholesale. She sought further assistance in marketing from the *Magazine of Direct Marketing* (Garden City, New York). Janet then put all the pieces together, her own ability to sell a product through advertising copy, a good product, and the direct-marketing techniques, to create a small, thriving business that has now expanded into a full jewelry and accessory line.

The world of business is as varied as your interests. Most businesses, even the multimillion-dollar corporations, began as a gleam in somebody's eye. Who would have believed ten years ago that natural foods and vitamins would become big business; that hand-made products would make such a comeback; that the little catering store around the corner would emerge as a major food vendor? Whenever the federal government grants money for a new project, private enterprise profits. School lunches, lunches on wheels for the elderly, institutional lunches are in some cases prepared at large commissaries or by an entrepreneur. Often training in a particular skill or industry will lead to opening a business. Whether your training lies in cosmetology or small appliance repair, going into business for yourself can be an exhilarating and rewarding experience. In your own business, your disability is certainly no handicap. You make the rules, the adjustments, the adaptations.

Franchising

You may feel that starting from scratch is too threatening a prospect. Consider franchising, but consider it carefully. There are a good many organizations willing to sell their name and not much else for a goodly sum of money. If you do decide to go the franchising route, choose an organization with a well-established reputation. Research carefully what your contribution will be and what the organization will contract to do. Franchising commitments in the food industry, for example, vary from sharing recipes for food preparation to marketing a finished product that is prepared at a central location. Whether the product is food, gas, human services, specialty shops, supermarkets or whatever, you need to do your homework before committing time and money to the venture.

Depending upon the nature of the company you will receive, in return for the purchase of franchising rights, the use of the name, benefits from local and national advertising, quality control, advice on management techniques and current information on the market place. More descriptive information can be had from the Internal Franchise Association, 7315 Wisconsin Avenue, Suite 600W, Washington, D.C. 20014, and from Stephen E. Goodman, Franchise Information Institute, P.O. Box 304, Dunellen, New Jersey 08812. These publications may also be helpful:

- Directory of Franchising Opportunities, Pilot Books, 347 Fifth Ave., New York, N.Y. 10016. Provides a description of six hundred firms and includes approximate investment.

- Franchise Digest, Ltd., Department IJA, P.O. Box 55, Ryder Station, Brooklyn, New York. A three-month trial subscription is $5.00.

Marketing Business Resources

Direct-mail advertising can be one of the least expensive and most profitable of your methods for marketing a product. Indeed, for you, direct mail can be the ideal method. At present writing, direct-mail sales average about $80 billion a year. Obviously this method is excellent for merchandising your goods. The Direct Mail Association, 6 East 42nd Street, New York, New York

10019, offers courses in a number of cities throughout the United States. They will also give information about the more than thirty colleges and universities that offer courses in the field. You may apply as well for a scholarship if you are interested in further study in the subject. In any event, write to them for more information.

Trade Journals

Another important resource for any entrepreneur is the trade journal and/or magazine. There is virtually a trade journal for every industry. Depending upon the size of the industry, there may be two or more competing journals. These journals are invaluable guides for the individual who is starting up a business as well as one who is already in business. Articles are written by experts in the particular industry. Trends are evaluated. Authorities offer their opinions on the effect of both national and international policy on the economics of marketing your product.

Trade Associations

Connected with many industries are specific trade associations. These organizations may be formed through union membership or by members of the field banding together to form an association. Usually a trade association, in addition to providing its membership with literature and news on the latest trends in the field, newsletters and journals, will hold an annual meeting. At this meeting, along with election of new officers, activities such as management workshops will be arranged for those members who want to learn more about techniques that have worked for colleagues in the industry. You might find this kind of conference quite profitable if you are contemplating starting a business in a particular industry.

Professional Assistance

In addition to the assistance that SBA can give you, it is important that you consider professional assistance. Whatever the size, every business must conform to a myriad of local, state and federal laws. Therefore, from the start, hire a professional accountant and attorney. Your accountant will set up your bookkeeping system to include an accounts receivable and accounts payable ledger, an inventory control and a billing system. You will be advised on what insurance to carry, how to register your business with the Internal Revenue Service and how to prepare for your tax return. Finding an accountant is relatively simple. Your friends, relatives, business associates, college, or if necessary the yellow pages can help you to locate a suitable candidate. Since the accounting procedures for small businesses are similar across a number of industries, you need not insist on an accountant with experience in your field.

Your attorney will help you to decide the business forms most appropriate for you and will draft the necessary documents. There are many forms a business can take, but the most appropriate for a small business should be one of the following: individual proprietorship, partnership, or a corporation.

Before you actually set up your business, examine the advantages and disadvantages of each business form. Take an active part in the decision. Your attorney or accountant should be able to provide you with enough information to help you understand the ramifications of each form. Remember that your accountant and attorney are in your employ, and it is their responsibility to assist you in making the best decision for setting up your business.

HOME WORK

Operating out of your home is a concept that is gaining respect and power. Although you may cling to the mainstream, you may want to investigate as have a great many individuals, handicapped and nonhandicapped, Alvin Toffler's predictions in *The Third Wave*. Toffler believes that despite the lure of industrialization, small-scale specialists will rise to the forefront. Economics is apparently partially responsible for this movement back to the cottage industry. With the sky-rocketing costs of corporate expenses on the management level and the expense and difficulty of commuting on the worker level, it again makes sense to consider small, local industries.

Two possibilities exist for working at home. On the one hand it is possible to create a one-person business similar to the businesses suggested in chapter 11. On the other hand independence may lie in becoming a contractor or off-site employee of a manufacturing concern.

Advantages and disadvantages are present in both possibilities. On the credit side you will within the confines of your own home, be able to conduct a business or work for a manufacturer. You need not contend with the travel difficulties, nor with adjustments and adaptations on the job, you can work at any time of the day or night, rest whenever you need to, eat nutritious lunches at minimal cost, and don't have to worry about an extensive wardrobe. You will also be able to set your speed of work, develop your own rhythm, work at your own pace, and if you are caring for another person, do so with little extra expense or inconvenience.

The debit side may include inadequate income, concern about the success of your work or your business, feelings of loneliness, no promotions if you are your own boss, and a certain amount of anxiety about the effect of current economic situations on your business.

Unquestionably, the above is only a sampling of the advantages and disadvantages of working at home. When you have thoroughly explored this alternative it is possible that your ledger will balance—that this arrangement is the most felicitous for you. Should this be your decision, investigate some of the possibilities available to you.

The Home Employee

There are a good number of industries that find it profitable to contract work to individuals at home. Some manufacturers actually install machines in the individual's home, using it as an adjunct to the factory. At present writing, however, there does not seem to be one source to which you can turn for a listing of those manufacturers. This information is apparently difficult to gather; since many of the businesses that contract out work are also small business operators, and since there are some twelve million owners of small business operating throughout the country, even a small percentage of those who would contract work out would still constitute a sizeable number. Your best bet, therefore, is to ask around, check with your friends and acquaintances, watch the local advertisements, place an ad in "situations wanted," write to your local chamber of commerce for a list of manufacturers operating in your area. You might also check the Yellow Pages and compile your own mailing list. When you have a suitable mailing list, develop a letter that can be sent to these manufacturers, stating your abilities and qualifications. You might investigate also the local chapters of your organizations, your state office of vocational rehabilitation, and any other government and nonprofit organizations involved in serving the disabled. Let it be known that you are available for work in the home.

At present, the Employment Standards Administration of the United States Department of Labor is seeking deregulation of the federal law that restricts homework in the industries of women's apparel, jewelry, knitted outerwear, gloves and mittens, buttons and buckles, handkerchiefs and embroideries. These restrictions were established forty years ago when it was discovered that these particular industries were a threat to maintaining labor standards. However, provision was made at that time, and it still exists today, that if you are handicapped and cannot adjust to factory work, or need to remain at home to care for an invalid, you are exempted from the law. You may also be employed in the restricted industries if you are under the supervision of a state vocational rehabilitation agency or a sheltered workshop.

While you may be unaffected by the deregulation of these seven industries, it is important to understand that the reason for regulation was for your protection under the Federal Minimum Wage Law. If your rights to a minimum wage are violated, you can file a complaint against your employer. Previously, within the restricted industries, if a complainant filed a grievance, the regulations did not assure payment of minimum wage, but in fact denied the complainant the right to work for less than minimum wage.

The kind of work you can do at home will vary according to the industry in your area. In Vermont, for example, manufacturers of knitted caps and mittens have used workers at home for many years. The industries previously mentioned obviously extend their production into the home. However, these industries are only the tip of the iceberg. You might find that takeout foods are gaining in popularity in your area. Many of the caterers, delicatessens, food emporiums, health food stores, charcuteries are now buying specialty food items from home kitchens. Your particular skill in needlecrafts or handicrafts may find a ready market. Your area may be in the midst of an economic upswing. Skilled technicians may be difficult to obtain, and the industry may turn to home workers for added personnel. Your competence with computers may result in your home becoming the site of a computer terminal where you can process one or more company's billing systems. A visit or phone call to the production manager of a growing organization might well yield a job that can be done as easily off as on the premises.

Some unusual sources of jobs in the home include becoming an advertising monitor for television. You need no skills nor investment. The money you make can be regarded as supplemental, since it pays about $100 a week, but you work only one week of each month monitoring programs on television. If you're interested, contact: Broadcast Advertisers Report, Chestnut and Fifth, Darby, Pennsylvania 19023. Try "Gallup polling" if you're able to use a telephone. To conduct a poll, you call persons from a list of names, ask them questions from a questionnaire developed by the polling company and write down the answers to those questions on your questionnaire. Many market research firms conduct a number of surveys for their clients. Check your local phone directory to see if there is a research organization in your area. The Princeton Survey Research Center at 53 Bank Street, Princeton, New Jersey 08550 can also supply you with information on sources.

There is a traditional source of home work associated with the creative individual. Writers write their books at home. Artists create their works in studios most often located in the home. Designers often begin their enterprise by working out of the home. Musicians use their homes for practice and instruction. Talent, it seems, is best fostered in the confines of one's own home. Often a particular talent can launch you on a productive career. Artistic ability may result in producing greeting cards, note paper, fabric designs. Writing may lend itself to freelance copywriting, proofreading, copyediting, writing articles, and so on. As a musician, you may be able to perform at children's parties, conventions, meetings and weddings. Whatever your talent, there appear to be a number of ways in which you can use it to bring about commercial success.

Other types of home work center around the ability to use a phone. Telephone soliciting ranging from selling magazine subscriptions to calling prospective clients, as does Mary M., a severely disabled woman, produces a small but steady income. The telephone company has specialized equipment for physically disabled persons. The equipment is adapted and modified to meet specific disability needs (see chapter 3). Mrs. Mary M. doesn't pay for the special equipment, only for the phone. With the money she earns, she is self-supporting. She does find the work monotonous at times, but the reward of becoming independent compensates for the tedium.

As with any endeavor, finding suitable home work will involve some effort on your part. Use some of the techniques you have learned from reading the preceding chapters of this book. Explore your resources. Contact all the important people who might be able to help you. Conduct a direct-mail campaign. Visit or phone promising industries. In other words, don't wait for the work to find you—go out there and get it.

Join the Cottage Industry Movement

Starting a business from your home is not unlike starting a small business (chapter 11). You may or may not need additional capital. You may or may not need additional space. You will certainly want to explore whatever assistance the Small Business Administration can give you. You will also want to evaluate the market to ascertain if your product and/or service is in demand.

The variety of small businesses people have started from their homes boggles the imagination. Ingenuity, inventiveness, coupled with a desire to work independently, appear to be the key motivating factors. Many home businesses have sprung from interests, hobbies and inventions. Others from expediency, necessity and fierce desire to work independently. Some businesses start out as an idea similar to that of Jean Nidetch, the founder of Weight Watchers, who simply felt the need to talk to other women who were undergoing the pressures of losing weight. When you begin to think about your own business examine your interests and talents first. Just about anything you like to do or are interested in can lead into a business venture. Consider some of the following ideas. After you examine them, we are sure that you will come up with dozens of your own.

If you like working with living things, however small and inarticulate, you might consider beekeeping. For an investment of about $20.00, you can get yourself a hive, veil, gloves and bees and set up your own honey-making factory. Like the idea? Read more about it in *How to Keep Bees and Sell Honey*, Walter T. Kelley, Walter T. Kelley Company, Clarkson, Kentucky 42720.

Or you might prefer earthworms. They take up little space, perform their functions out of sight and breed rapidly. Zoos, fisherpersons, gardeners, laboratories, aquariums all can become your customers. Again, the investment is small. You buy yourself a passel of worms, put them into rich, loamy soil, and presto, they'll start breeding. Just make sure they don't freeze.

If you are mobile, you might consider dog walking, dog and cat feeding, plant watering, house sitting or a combination of one or more of these activities. Many people who vacation now prefer to have a reliable individual feed and walk their animals and take care of their homes. You can usually find out the going rate for these services through asking around in your community. As you build a reputation for reliability and efficiency, you can set your own rates.

Every Easter, white and yellow fluff descends upon us like the gentle rains of spring. Chicks and bunnies are eagerly sought as Easter gifts. If you have the space and temperament, you might want to try your hand at animal husbandry. The raising of chickens and rabbits can become a productive meat, poultry and egg business as well.

Mechanically inclined? All those machines that sit on counters—all that audiovisual equipment toted about on backs and shoulders, break down. If you're handy with tools, have a natural ability to understand the principles of mechanics, there's a market in small appliance or audiovisual repair for you. To become adept at the skill, we suggest you take one or more courses at a community college, trade or technical school. Your local office of vocational rehabilitation will be able to help you get the training you need. When you have the skills, set up a shop in your home, advertise locally, let friends know about your services, and soon you'll find that your reputation is outpacing your capacity to repair all the items that come your way.

This same philosophy applies to those of you who have the ability to sew. Sewing naturally lends itself to a small business operation. A hand-sewn garment is considered a rarity today. Even with the plethora of ready-to-wear clothes a number of women still want a dressmaker to fashion a very special dress or suit. Historically, the seamstress has held a special place in society. Before the advent of industrialization, tailoring was largely conducted from the home. One of the authors of this book recalls hearing how her mother supported herself in Russia during the eight years her father was in the United States building a new home. Mother was an excellent seamstress and finding herself on her own, started a small business, eventually employing two seamstresses to keep up with the flow of orders.

An ability to sew may develop into a number of other activities. Doll repair combines sewing and minimal mechanical skills. Upholstery combines sewing, mechanical and some carpentry skills. If you have a sewing skill, enjoy sewing, then examine the many possibilities available for turning that skill into a business.

Good with figures? Try income tax preparation. You'll need to a take a course at a community college or with an organization such as H & R Block. The work is seasonal but lucrative. The H & R Block Tax Training Institute is at 4410 Main Street, Kansas City, Missouri 64111.

How about gardening? You can grow, dry and package your own herbs. Herbs are gaining in popularity as many people on a low-sodium diet are turning to these zesty seasonings as substitutes for salt. For more information, read *Herbs: Their Culture and Use,* Rosetta E. Clarkson, Macmillan, Inc., 866 Third Avenue, New York, New York 10022.

Good organizational skills? Stella McBride, whose organizing skills were winning her plaudits on her job, decided to set out on her own. She called her local TV station and told them she was starting an unusual business, contacted the newspapers in her area who, intrigued by the idea, ran stories on her. Through these sources she began to attract clients. Basically, Stella found, people were dismayed and ashamed at the chaos they had created or which had been created by others, and were only too pleased to have a consultant help them organize their affairs. Stella's business extends from home to business organization.

Persuasive? Try your hand at selling. Telephone sales, door-to-door sales, direct-mail sales. A good salesperson can sell anything from insurance to toys. If the product you choose to represent is nationally advertised, your selling job should be relatively easy.

What's your office skill ability? Typing, bookkeeping, tax work provide a number of possibilities for small home businesses. Many freelance typists, for example, are considered invaluable assets to professional writers and graduate students. They turn out perfectly typed manuscripts according to accepted journalistic or academic style. If you can also copy edit, you can boost the fees. Should you plan this enterprise, get yourself several books on style, such as *Words into Type,* Skillin and Gay, Prentice-Hall, Inc., Englewood Cliffs, New Jersey 07632; and *The Chicago Manual of Style,* University of Chicago Press, Chicago, Illinois 60637.

Creative? Try your hand with puppets. If you can make your own, you can save the cost of purchasing them. Puppeteering includes the use of just about every creative skill you possess:

writing scripts, designing puppets and screens, acting, singing. If you are homebound, you might want to limit yourself to making puppets. However, if you can travel about, try some puppet performances. Puppeteering is an old-time art that is regaining popularity. Witness the Muppets. You may be familiar with the "Kids on the Block" project. This is a puppet show where handicapped puppets talk about problems that center largely on getting the nonhandicapped to realize that differences are minimal. This project has gained wide acceptance with the educational community. Your own ideas and ingenuity might help you to produce a similar activity.

Inventive? At times your creativity may extend to turning found materials (seeds, acorns, flowers, packing materials, throwaways) into art collages, boutique items or items for practical use. Or you may be the kind of person who enjoys solving problems through developing or inventing new products. If you really feel that you have a product that is worth marketing, get in touch with Maggie Weisberg, vice-president of the Inventors Workshop International and Inventors Licensing and Marketing Agency. She has built her own small business from helping inventors to market their products. She will help you to patent your invention, market it and set up your business. The address is Maggie Weisberg, Inventors Licensing and Marketing Agency, Tarzana, California 91356.

If you prefer to work on your own, get in touch with a patent attorney. Be sure to set the fee in advance. Attempting to market your product to a large company may be difficult since most companies have their own research and development departments. You may, therefore, decide to go it alone. If it is saleable and is the right product at the right time, then by all means strike out on your own.

How To: How-to books seem to find a steady market. If you have a particular skill or ability, you may want to write a book telling other people how to do it. Not every book finds a publisher, however. A number of individuals have taken the risk and published their own books confirming a hunch about a ready market. Arthur Frommer (*Europe on $5 a Day*) published his first book independently. Recipe collections which began life as mimeographed sheets, have ended up as nicely bound hardcover editions. Before you invest time and effort in launching a series of how-to books, explore both the market and your financial stretch. You will need to sustain yourself without immediate income as you research and write your first how-to book.

A Word of Caution

Deal only with reputable firms, and carefully investigate ads that want you to send in sums of money. Jobs addressing envelopes may be a fraud.

Avoid the "easy riches" ads, and the fantastic new product ads that will net you thousands in only ten hours a week of working time.

Avoid publishing ads that promise to make your book a bestseller. All you do is underwrite the cost of publication.

If in doubt, check with the Better Business Bureau, the state labor department and consumer protection agencies.

If you have succumbed to the glories of becoming rich overnight and find yourself the victim of fraud, complain loudly. Most newspapers and magazines do not wittingly take on "come-on" advertising.

Some sources that may prove helpful are:

- *On Your Own—99 Alternatives to a 9–5 Job,* Kathy Mathews, Random House, 1979.

- *Small Business Index,* Wayne D. Kryszak, The Scarecrow Press, Metuchen, New Jersey, 1978. An index to American and Canadian books, pamphlets and periodicals that contain information on starting small businesses. Materials listed in the index vary in length from a page or two to complete books. A helpful guide for persons seriously contemplating working at home or starting a small business.

- *Home Study Opportunities,* (free pamphlet), B'nai B'rith Career and Counseling Service, 1640 Rhode Island Ave., N.W., Washington, D.C. 20036.

- *The Family Circle Book of Careers at Home,* Mary Bess Gilson, Cowles Book Company, 1971.

THERESA STRATTHAUS

"In a few years I hope to get my Ph.D.," Theresa tosses off nonchalantly. Expecting to get a Ph.D. by the age of thirty-five is no big deal, but for Theresa, who was diagnosed as mentally retarded as soon as she entered school, obtaining the ultimate degree is a dream she hopes to make come true.

It hasn't been easy. During her first three years in elementary school, Theresa played the role of "dummy," believing that she was unable to communicate and learn because she was just too dumb to absorb information. Fortunately, she was sent to a speech teacher, who upon observing her became convinced that her problem was neither one of retardation nor of emotional disturbance, but might possibly be caused by some physical factor. He advised the school authorities to have Theresa's hearing tested. It was found that Theresa had a severe hearing impairment. The pain and dizziness she had complained about were at last diagnosed.

Therein began Theresa's first educational step. Her speech teacher, sensing that beneath the feisty, awkward exterior there was an untapped intelligence, voluntarily taught her what had by-passed her during those early elementary years.

From that point on, was it easy? Unfortunately, Theresa's story doesn't follow a story-book formula. In junior high school she was placed in a special education class, a decision that undid the positive effects of her association with her speech teacher. Theresa, now a vigorous teenager, slid into the drug scene, emerging deaf from the experience. After a stint at Topic House, a drug treatment facility, she was fired with a new determination—to get an education.

With the help of tutors she completed the requirements for her high school equivalency diploma. Ready for higher education, she contacted OVR, and together with her counselor decided on Nassau Community College, but within the first semester, her old problems surfaced, and she dropped out. Her next try, the State University at Old Westbury, a new institution founded on the premise of providing educational opportunity to the nontraditional student, proved more felicitous. She was graduated with a double major in psychology and communications and creative arts. A year later, she crammed a two-year art course into one year, gaining a master's degree from C.W. Post College. By this time her talent for creating art objects became readily apparent and she earned an A.A.S. degree from the Fashion Institute of Technology, winning the outstanding jewelry designer of the year award. At present, she is completing her M.S. in community psychological counseling. And she doesn't intent to stop her education until she has her Ph.D.

To support herself, she works part-time using both her skills in art and in counseling. She has a job in a youth center for troubled adolescents and has worked as an art instructor on the college level and as an art therapist for students with special needs.

CONCLUSION

Why work? Why indeed? Just as the need for work, "The Search for Dignity," reverberates through the many interviews, correspondence and literature on job hunting for persons with disabilities, so does another element, that of disincentives, echo a countermessage. As a result of your disability you may be receiving a number of entitlements, i.e., SST, social security disability, insurance disability, and various other entitlements depending upon your particular handicap. The sum of these entitlements may bring you enough money to live on. Why work then? Why throw yourself into the mainstream day after day, pit yourself against what at times appear to be overwhelming odds for the sake of earning a salary that in the end may be no greater in take-home pay than what you have been receiving from your entitlements?

Talking with you who do work, who have found ways to contribute productively to society, the answer is—there's no other way. The Talmud elevates work as one of man's most worthwhile pursuits; Freud added love to work as the mark of the emotionally healthy individual. You yourself, in the many ways you have demonstrated through your undaunted quest for a job, have told us that, in the words of Paul Sottnek, work is "a search for dignity."

PUBLICATIONS OF THE NATIONAL CENTER ON EMPLOYMENT OF THE HANDICAPPED

The National Center on Employment of the Handicapped at Human Resources Center, I.U. Willets Road, Albertson, New York 11507, has published a number of books and pamphlets that should prove valuable. Below is a selected list of some of the titles. Write to them for their complete catalogue.

Hand Controls and Assistive Devices for the Physically Disabled Driver; 60 pages, $5.00.

No. 1 General Information to Help the Recently Disabled; 24 pages, $2.50.

No. 4 Vocational and Educational Opportunities for the Disabled; 36 pages, $2.50.

Work Independence and the Severely Disabled: A Bibliography; 108 pages, $7.50.

Modifying the Work Environment for the Physically Disabled; 128 pages, $8.95.

Modifying the Work Environment for the Physically Disabled Employee; parts 1 and 2; 128 pages, $16.65.

Books by Henry Viscardi, Jr., President Emeritus and founder of Human Resources Center:

The Abilities Story, $6.95; *But not on Our Block,* $6.95; *Give Us the Tools,* $8.95; *A Laughter in the Lonely Night,* $5.00; *A Man's Stature,* $6.95.

SOURCES OF ASSISTANCE—FEDERAL AGENCIES

National Offices

U.S. Equal Employment
  Opportunity Commission
Washington, D.C. 20506

Office for Civil Rights
U.S. Department of Health and
  Human Services
Washington, D.C. 20201

Social Security Administration
U.S. Department of Health and
  Human Services
Washington, D.C. 20201

Internal Revenue Service
U.S. Department of the
  Treasury
Washington, D.C. 20224

Pension Benefit Guaranty
  Corp.
2020 K Street, N.W.
Washington, D.C. 20006

Labor-Management Services
  Administration
U.S. Department of Labor
Washington, D.C. 20210

Office of Federal Contract
  Compliance Programs
Employment Standards
  Administration
U.S. Department of Labor
Washington, D.C. 20210

Women's Bureau
Office of the Secretary
U.S. Department of Labor
Washington, D.C. 20210

Wage and Hour Division
Employment Standards
  Administration
U.S. Department of Labor
Washington, D.C. 20210

APPENDIX III

RELEVANT ORGANIZATIONS

A partial listing of organizations that can provide information on jobs, educational opportunities and which also advocate for the rights of persons with handicapping conditions. The majority of these organizations hold annual conferences and publish newsletters and journals where job openings in your field may be listed.

Advocates for the Handicapped
2200 Merchandise Mart
Chicago, Illinois 60654
  313- 822-0435
  Pub.   *The Advocate*

Alexander Graham Bell
  Association for the Deaf
3417 Volta Place, N.W.
Washington, D.C. 20007
  202-337-5220
  Pub.   *Newsounds*

American Association of the
  Deaf Blind
Chicago Lighthouse for the
  Blind
1850 W. Roosevelt Road
Chicago, Illinois 60608
  312- 666-1331
  Pub.   *The Voice*

American Association of
  Workers for the Blind
1511 K St., N.W.
Washington, D.C. 20005
  202- 347-1559
  Pub.   *News & Views*
            Blindness

American Brotherhood for the
  Blind
National Center for the Blind
1800 Johnson Street
Baltimore, Maryland 21230
  301-659-9315
  Pub.   *Hot Line to Deaf-*
            Blind

American Cancer Society
777 Third Avenue
New York, New York 10017
  212-371-2900
  Pub.   *World Smoking &*
            Health
            Cancer: Journal of the
            American Society

American Coalition of Citizens
with Disabilities
1200 15th Street N.W., Suite 20
Washington, D.C. 20005
202-785-4268
Pub.   *Achievement,*
National Voice
of Disabled
The Coalition

American Council of the Blind
1211 Connecticut Avenue
N.W., Suite 506
Washington, D.C. 20036
202-833-1251
Pub.   *The Braille Forum*

American Congress of
Rehabilitative Medicine
30 N. Michigan Avenue,
Suite 922
Chicago, Illinois 60602
312-236-9512
Pub.   *Rehab Congress*
News

American Deafness and
Rehabilitation Association
814 Thayer Avenue
Silver Springs, Maryland
20910; 301-589-0880
Pub.   *A.D.A.R.A.*
Newsletter

American Diabetes Association
600 Fifth Avenue, 8th Floor
New York, New York 10020
212-541-4310
Pub.   *Diabetes Forecast*

American Foundation for the
Blind
15 West 16th Street
New York, New York 10011
212-620-2000
Pub.   *Braille Research*
Newsletter
Journal of Visual
Impairment and
Blindness
Washington Report

American Heart Association
7320 Greenville Avenue
Dallas, Texas 75231

American Lung Association
1740 Broadway
New York, New York 10019
212-245-8000
Pub.   *American Lung*
Association
Bulletin

American Occupational
Therapy Association
1383 Piccard Drive
Rockville, Maryland 20850
301-962-9626
Pub.   *American Journal*
of Occupational
Therapy
Occupational
Therapy
Newsletter

American Orthotic and
Prosthetic Association
1444 N Street, N.W.
Washington, D.C. 20005
202-234-8400
Pub.   *The Almanac*
Newsletter
Orthotics and Prosthetics

American Physical Therapy
Association
1156 15th St. N.W., Suite 500
Washington, D.C. 20005
202-466-2070
Pub.   *Physical Therapy
Progress Report*

American Speech, Language,
Hearing Association
10801 Rockville Pike
Rockville, Maryland 20852
301-897-5700
Pub.   *Journal of Speech
& Hearing
Disorders*

Amyotrophic Lateral Sclerosis
Society of America
15300 Ventura Boulevard,
Suite 30
Sherman Oaks, California
91403; 213-990-2151
Pub.   *The Alssoan*

Arthritis Foundation
3400 Peachtree Road N.E.,
Suite 1101
Atlanta, Georgia 30326
404-266-0795
Pub.   *Arthritis News*

Association for Children with
Learning Disabilities
(Learning Disabilities Adult
Committee)
4156 Library Road
Pittsburgh, Pennsylvania 15234
412-231-7977
Pub.   *LDAC Newsletter
News Briefs*

Association for the Education
of the Visually Handicapped
919 Walnut Street, 4th Floor
Philadelphia, Pennsylvania
19107; 215-923-7155
Pub.   *Education of the
Visually
Handicapped
Fountainhead*

Association for the Severely
Handicapped
1600 West Armory Way
Seattle, Washington 98119
206-283-5055
Pub.   *TASH Newsletter*

Better Hearing Institute
1430 K Street, N.W., Suite 600
Washington, D.C. 20005
202-638-7577
Pub.   *The
Communicator*

Blinded Veterans Association
1735 DeSales Street N.W.
Washington, D.C. 20036
202-347-4010
Pub.   *The BVA Bulletin*

Braille Institute of America
741 North Vermont Avenue
Los Angeles, California 90029
213-663-1111
Pub.   *The Braille Mirror*

Closer Look
1201 16th Street N.W., Suite
606E
Washington, D.C. 20036
202-833-4160
Pub.   *Closer Look
Common Sense*

Consumers Organization for
the Hearing Impaired
P.O. Box 166
Owings Mills, Maryland 21117
301-593-3587
Pub.   *C.O.H.I. Reporter*

Cystic Fibrosis Foundation
3384 Peachtree Road N.E.,
Suite 875
Atlanta, Georgia 30326
404- 233-2195

Disabled American Veterans
807 Maine Avenue S.W.
Washington, D.C. 20024
202-554-3501
Pub.   *DAV*

Down's Syndrome Congress
1310 E. Heritage Rd.
Normal, Illinois 61761
309-452-3264

Emphysema Anonymous
P.O. Box 66
Fort Meyers, Florida 33902
813-334-4226
Pub.   *Batting the Breeze*

Epilepsy Foundation of
America
1828 L Street N.W., Room 406
Washington, D.C. 20036
202-293-2930
Pub.   *The National
Spokesman*

Foundation for Science and the
Handicapped
26827 Sturdy Oak Drive
Elkhart, Indiana 46514
219-264-7644
Pub.   *Newsletter*

Gallaudet College
7th & Florida Avenue N.E.
Washington, D.C. 20002
202-651-5000
Pub.   *Junior Deaf
American*

Helen Keller, International
20 West 17th Street
New York, New York 10011
212-620-2100
Pub.   *HKI Report*

Industry-Labor Council,
Human Resources Center
Albertson, New York 11507
516-747-5400
Pub.   *Industry-Labor
Council
Newsletter*

International Association of
Parents of the Deaf
814 Thayer Avenue
Silver Springs, Maryland
20910; 301-585-5400
Pub.   *The Endeavor*

International Association of
Laryngectomies
777 Third Avenue, 5th Floor
New York, New York 10017
212-371-2900
Pub.   *IAL News*

Jewish Braille Institute of
America
110 East 30th Street
New York, New York 10016
212-889-2525
Pub.   *Jewish Braille
Review*

Little People of America
P.O. Box 126
Owatonna, Minnesota 55060
570-451-3842
Pub.   *LPA News*

Lupus Foundation of America
11673 Holly Springs Drive
St. Louis, Missouri 63141
314-872-9036
Pub.   *Lupus News*

March of Dimes Birth Defects
   Foundation
1275 Mamaroneck Avenue
White Plains, New York 10605
914-428-7100
Pub.   *The Volunteer*

Menninger Foundation
P.O. Box 829
Topeka, Kansas 66601
913-234-9566
Pub.   *Bulletin of the*
       Menninger
       Clinic

Muscular Dystrophy
   Association
810 Seventh Avenue
New York, New York 10019
212-586-0808
Pub.   *MDA News*

Myesthenia Gravis Foundation
15 East 26th Street, Room 1603
New York, New York 10010
212-889-8157
Pub.   *Update*

National Amputation Foundation
12–45 150th Street
Whitestone, New York 11357
212-767-8400
Pub.   *The AMP*

National Association of the
   Deaf
814 Thayer Avenue
Silver Springs, Maryland
   20910; 301-587-1788
Pub.   *The Deaf*
       American
       The Broadcaster

National Association for the
   Deaf-Blind
2703 Forest Oak Circle
Norman, Oklahoma 73071
405-360-2580
Pub.   *Newsletter*

National Association of
   Patients on Hemodialysis and
   Transplantations
505 Northern Boulevard
Great Neck, New York 11021
516-482-2720
Pub.   *NAPHT News*

National Association of the
   Physically Handicapped
76 Elm Street
London, Ohio 43140
614-852-1664
Pub.   *NAPH National*
       Newsletter

National Association of
   Rehabilitation Facilities
5530 Wisconsin Avenue,
   Suite 955
Washington, D.C. 20015
301-654-5882

National Association for
   Retarded Citizens
P.O. Box 6109
Arlington, Texas 76011
817-261-4961
Pub.   *The ARC*

National Association for Sickle
Cell Disease
3460 Wilshire Boulevard,
Suite 1012
Los Angeles, California 90010
213-731-1166
Pub.   *Viewpoint*

National Association for the
Visually Handicapped
305 East 24th Street
New York, New York 10010
212-889-3141
Pub.   *In Focus*

National Braille Association
654-A Godwin Avenue
Midland, New Jersey 07432
201-447-1484
Pub.   *NBA Bulletin*

National Center for Law and
the Deaf
7th and Florida Avenue N.E.
Washington, D.C. 20002
202-651-5454
Pub.   *NCLD Newsletter*

National Congress of
Organizations of the
Physically Handicapped
16630 Beverly Avenue
Tinley Park, Illinois 60477
312-532-3566
Pub.   *COPH Bulletin*

National Council of Stutterers,
Speech and Hearing Clinics
Catholic University of America
Washington, D.C. 20064
202-635-5556
Pub.   *Journal*

National Easter Seal Society
for Crippled Children &
Adults
2023 West Ogden Avenue
Chicago, Illinois 60612
312-243-8400
Pub.   *Easter Seal
          Communicator
          Rehabilitation
          Literature*

National Federation of the
Blind
National Center for the Blind
1800 Johnson Street
Baltimore, Maryland 21230
301-659-9314
Pub.   *The Braille
          Monitor
          Job Bulletin*

National Hemophilia
Foundation
19 West 34th Street
New York, New York 10018
212-563-0211

National Kidney Foundation
2 Park Avenue
New York, New York 10016
212-889-2210

National Library Service for
Blind and Physically
Handicapped
Library of Congress
Washington, D.C. 20542
202-882-5500
Pub.   *Update
          Talking Book
          Topics*

National Mental Health
  Association
1800 North Kent Street,
  2nd Floor
Arlington, Virginia 22209
  703-528-6405
  Pub.   *In Touch*

National Multiple Sclerosis
  Society
205 East 42nd Street, 3rd Floor
New York, New York 10017
  212-986-3240
  Pub.   *M.S. Briefs*

National Spinal Cord Injury
  Foundation
369 Elliot Street
Newton Upper Falls,
  Massachusetts 02164
  617-964-0521
  Pub.   *Paraplegia Life*

National Rehabilitation
  Information Center
Catholic University of America
8th and Varnum Street N.E.
Washington, D.C. 20064
  202-635-5826
  Pub.   *The Pathfinder*

National Society to Prevent
  Blindness
79 Madison Avenue, 5th Floor
New York, New York 10016
  212-684-3505
  Pub.   *Prevent Blindness
              News
              Sightsaving
              Review*

National Tay Sachs Foundation
  and Allied Diseases
  Association
122 East 42nd Street
New York, New York 10017
  212-661-2780

The Orton Society
8415 Bellona Lane, Suite 113
Towson, Maryland 21204
  301-296-0232

Paralyzed Veterans of America
5201 North 19th Avenue,
  Suite 111
Phoenix, Arizona 85015
  602-246-9426
  Pub.   *Paraplegia News*

People to People
Committee for the
  Handicapped
1522 K Street N.W., Suite 1130
Washington, D.C. 20005
  202-638-2487
  Pub.   *Newsletter*

President's Committee on
  Employment of the
  Handicapped
1111 20th Street N.W.,
  Room 636
Washington, D.C. 20036
  202-653-5057
  Pub.   *Disabled USA*

Rehabilitation International,
  USA
20 West 40th Street
New York, New York 10018
  212-869-9907
  Pub.   *Rehabilitation
              World*

Rehabilitation Services
Administration
330 C Street S.W.
Washington, D.C.
(See state and local divisions
of vocational rehabilitation)

Spina Bifida Association of
America
343 South Dearborn Street,
Suite 319
Chicago, Illinois 60604
312-663-1562
Pub.   *The Pipeline*

Tourette Syndrome Association
42-40 Bell Boulevard
Bayside, New York 11361
212-224-2999
Pub.   *Newsletter*

United Cerebral Palsy
Association
66 East 34th Street
New York, New York 10016
212-481-6300
Pub.   *UC People, Etc.*
        Word from
        Washington

Ombudsman-Type Organizations

Disability Rights Center
1346 Connecticut Avenue N.W.
Suite 1124
Washington, D.C. 20036
202-223-3304

Mainstream, Inc.
1200 5th Street, N.W.
Washington, D.C. 20005
212-424-8089

Affirmative Action
Office of Federal Contract
Compliance
Department of Labor
Washington, D.C. 20210
202-655-4000

National Center on
Employment of the
Handicapped at Human
Resources Center
I. U. Willets Road
Albertson, New York 11507
516-747-5400

Untapped Resources, Inc.
60 First Avenue
New York, New York 10009
212-532-4422

APPENDIX IV

ON-THE-JOB TRAINING PROJECT OFFICES

National Project Office:
National Project Director
Association for Retarded Citizens National Headquarters
P.O. Box 6109
Arlington, Texas 76011
807-261-4961

STATES SERVED	FIELD COORDINATORS' LOCATIONS
Delaware Maryland Pennsylvania District of Columbia	5602 Baltimore National Pike Suite 307 Baltimore, Maryland 21228 301-744-0257
Texas Colorado Kansas New Mexico Oklahoma	P.O. Box 6109 Arlington, Texas 76011 817-261-4961
Minnesota Nebraska North Dakota South Dakota	1621 S. University Drive Suite 202 Fargo, North Dakota 58102 701-235-4479
Massachusetts Maine Vermont New Hampshire	377 Elliot Street Newton Upper Falls, Massachusetts 02164 617-964-4080
Connecticut New Jersey New York Rhode Island	99 Bayard Street New Brunswick, New Jersey 08901 201-246-2525

STATES SERVED	FIELD COORDINATORS' LOCATIONS
Nevada California Arizona Utah	401 South 3rd Street Suite 312 Las Vegas, Nevada 89101 702-384-5988
Alabama Florida Georgia South Carolina Tennessee	2815 Clearview Place Suite 500 Atlanta, Georgia 30340 404-458-8024
Arkansas Louisiana Mississippi Missouri	Woodland Hills Building 3000 Old Canton Road Suite 585 Jackson, Mississippi 39216 601-362-7912
Illinois Indiana Ohio Iowa Michigan Wisconsin	2700 Laura Lane Middleton, Wisconsin 53562 608-831-1151
Alaska Idaho Montana Oregon Washington Wyoming	5707 Lacey Boulevard Suite 109 Lacey, Washington 98503 206-491-3141
Kentucky North Carolina Virginia West Virginia	827 East Main Street Suite 1803 Richmond, Virginia 23219 804-649-9650

FEDERAL EMPLOYMENT JOB INFORMATION CENTERS

These Job Information Centers provide information with regard to federal employment. Some centers may also provide information about other jurisdictions (city, county or state). Information specialists are on hand to assist you in learning more about those jobs that are available, and the procedures for applying for them.

Alabama
Southerland Building
806 Governors Drive N.W.
Huntsville, Alabama 35801
205-453-5070

Alaska
Federal Building & U.S.
Courthouse
701 C Street, P.O. Box 22
Anchorage, Alaska 99513
907-271-5821

Arizona
522 North Central Avenue
Phoenix, Arizona 85004
602-261-4736

Arkansas
Federal Building
700 West Capitol Avenue,
Room 1319
Little Rock, Arkansas 72201

California
Linder Building
845 South Figueroa
Los Angeles, California
90017
213-688-3360

Federal Building
650 Capitol Mall
Sacramento, California 95814
916-440-3441

880 Front Street
San Diego, California 92188
714-293-6165

Federal Building
450 Golden Gate Avenue,
Room 1001
San Francisco, California
94102
415-556-6667

Colorado
1845 Sherman Street
Denver, Colorado 80203
303-837-3506

Connecticut
Federal Building
450 Main Street, Room 717
Hartford, Connecticut 06103
203-244-3096

Delaware
Federal Building
844 King Street
Wilmington, Delaware 19801
302-571-6288

District of Columbia
1900 E Street, N.W.
Washington, D.C. 20415
202-737-9616

Florida
1000 Brickell Avenue,
Suite 660
Miami, Florida, 33131
305-350-4725

80 North Hughey Avenue
Orlando, Florida 32801
305-420-6148

Georgia
Richard B. Russell Federal
Building
75 Spring Street S.W.
Atlanta, Georgia 30303
404-221-4315

Guam
238 O'Hara Street
Room 308
Agana, Guam 96910
344-5242

Hawaii
Federal Building
300 Ala Moana Boulevard,
Room 1310
Honolulu, Hawaii 96850
808-546-8600

Idaho
Box 035, Federal Building
550 West Fort Street
Boise, Idaho 83724
208-384-1726

Illinois
Dirksen Building
219 South Dearborn Street,
Room 1322
Chicago, Illinois 60604
312-353-5136

Indiana
46 East Ohio Street,
Room 123
Indianapolis, Indiana 46204
317-269-7161/7162

Iowa
210 Walnut Street, Room 191
Des Moines, Iowa 50309
515-284-4546

Kansas
One-Twenty Building
120 South Market Street,
Room 101
Wichita, Kansas 67202
316-267-6311, x106

Kentucky
Federal Building
600 Federal Plaza
Louisville, Kentucky 40202
502-582-5130

Louisiana
F. Edward Hebert Building
610 South Street, Room 103
New Orleans, Louisiana
70130
504-589-2764

Maine
Federal Building
Sewall Street & Western
Avenue, Room 611
Augusta, Maine 04330
207-622-6171, x269

Maryland
Garmatz Federal Building
101 West Lombard Street
Baltimore, Maryland 21201
301-962-3822

Massachusetts
3 Center Plaza
Boston, Massachusetts 02108
617-233-2571

Michigan
477 Michigan Avenue,
Room 595
Detroit, Michigan 48226
313-226-6950

Minnesota
Federal Building
Fort Snelling,
Twin Cities, Minnesota 55111
612-725-3355

Mississippi
100 West Capitol Street,
Suite 102
Jackson, Mississippi 39201
601-969-4585

Missouri
Federal Building
601 East 12th Street,
Room 129
Kansas City, Missouri 64106
816-374-5702

Federal Building
1520 Market Street,
Room 1712
St. Louis, Missouri 63103
314-425-4285

Montana
Federal Building and
Courthouse
301 South Park, Room 153
Helena, Montana 59601
406-449-5388

Nebraska
U.S. Courthouse and Post
Office Building
215 North 17th Street,
Room 1014
Omaha, Nebraska 68102
402-221-3815

Nevada
Mill and South Virginia
Streets
P.O. Box 3296
Reno, Nevada 89505
702-784-5535

New Hampshire
Federal Building
Daniel and Penhallow
Streets, Room 104
Portsmouth, New Hampshire
03801
603-436-7720, x762

New Jersey
Federal Building
970 Broad Street
Newark, New Jersey 07102
201-645-3673

Camden: 215-597-7440

New Mexico
Federal Building
421 Gold Avenue S.W.
Albuquerque, New Mexico
87102
505-766-2557

New York
590 Grand Concourse
Bronx, New York 10451
212-292-4666

111 West Huron Street,
Room 35
Buffalo, New York 14202
716-846-4001

90-04-161st Street, Room 200
Jamaica, New York 11432
212-526-6192

Federal Building
26 Federal Plaza
New York, New York 10007
212-264-0422

100 South Clinton Street
Syracuse, New York 13260
315-423-5660

North Carolina
Federal Building
310 New Bern Avenue
P.O. Box 25069
Raleigh, North Carolina
27611
919-755-4361

North Dakota
Federal Building
657 Second Avenue North,
Room 202
Fargo, North Dakota 58102
701-237-5771, x363

Ohio
Federal Building
1240 East 9th Street
Cleveland, Ohio 44199
216-522-4232

Federal Building Lobby
200 West 2nd Street
Dayton, Ohio 45402
513-225-2720/2854

Oklahoma
700 N.W. Fifth Street
Oklahoma City, Oklahoma
73102
405-231-4948

Oregon
Federal Building
1220 S.W. Third Street,
Lobby (North)
Portland, Oregon 97204
503-221-3141

Pennsylvania
Federal Building, Room 168
Harrisburg, Pennsylvania
17108
717-782-4494

William J. Green, Jr. Federal
Building
600 Arch Street
Philadelphia, Pennsylvania
19106
215-597-7440

Federal Building
1000 Liberty Avenue
Pittsburgh, Pennsylvania
15222
412-644-2755

Puerto Rico
Frederico Degetau Federal
Building
Carlos E. Chardon Street
San Juan,
Hato Rey, Puerto Rico 00918
809-753-4200, x209

Rhode Island
Federal and P.O. Building
Kennedy Plaza, Room 310
Providence, Rhode Island
02903
401-528-4447

South Carolina
Federal Building
334 Meeting Street
Charleston, South Carolina
29403
803-724-4328

South Dakota
Federal Building
U.S. Court House
515 9th Street, Room 201
Rapid City, South Dakota
57701
605-348-2221

Tennessee
Federal Building
167 North Main Street
Memphis, Tennessee 38103
901-521-3956

Texas
1100 Commerce Street,
Room 1C42
Dallas, Texas 75242
214-749-7721

Property Trust Building
2211 East Missouri Avenue,
Suite N302
El Paso, Texas 79903
915-543-7425

702 Caroline Street
Houston, Texas 77002
713-226-5501

643 East Durango Boulevard
San Antonio, Texas 78205
512-229-6600

Utah
350 South Main Street,
Room 484
Salt Lake City, Utah 84101
801-524-5744

Vermont
Federal Building
P.O. Box 489
Elmwood Avenue and Pearl
Street, Room 614
Burlington, Vermont 05402
802-862-6712

Virginia
Federal Building
200 Granby Mall, Room 220
Norfolk, Virginia 23510
804-441-3355

Washington
Federal Building
915 Second Avenue
Seattle, Washington 98174
206-442-4365

West Virginia
Federal Building
500 Quarrier Street
Charleston, West Virginia
25301
304-343-6181, x226

Wisconsin
Plankinton Building
161 West Wisconsin Avenue,
Room 205
Milwaukee, Wisconsin 53203
414-244-3761

Wyoming
2120 Capitol Avenue, Room
304
P.O. Box 967
Cheyenne, Wyoming 82001
307-778-2220, x2108

REGIONAL OFFICES— BUREAU OF APPRENTICESHIP AND TRAINING

Boston: JKF Federal Building, Government Center, Room 1001, Boston, Massachusetts 02203; 617-223-6740.

For Connecticut, Maine, Massachusetts, New Hampshire, Rhode Island and Vermont.

New York: 1515 Broadway and 44th Street, New York, New York 10036; 212-944-3061.

For New Jersey, New York, Puerto Rico and the Virgin Islands.

Philadelphia: Gateway Building, 3535 Market Street, Room 13240, Philadelphia, Pennsylvania 19104; 215-596-6417.

For Delaware, District of Columbia, Maryland, Pennsylvania, Virginia and West Virginia.

Atlanta: 1371 Peachtree Street N.E., Room 700, Atlanta, Georgia 30367; 404-881-4405.

For Alabama, Florida, Georgia, Kentucky, Mississippi, North Carolina, South Carolina and Tennessee.

Chicago: 230 South Dearborn Street, 7th Floor, Column #5, Chicago, Illinois 60604; 312-353-7205.

For Illinois, Indiana, Michigan, Minnesota, Ohio and Wisconsin.

Dallas: 555 Griffin Square Building, Dallas, Texas 75202; 214-767-4993.

For Arkansas, Louisiana, New Mexico, Oklahoma and Texas.

Kansas City: 1100 Federal Office Building, 911 Walnut Street, Kansas City, Missouri 64106; 816-374-3856.

For Iowa, Kansas, Missouri and Nebraska.

Denver: U.S. Custom House, 721 19th-Street, Room 476, Denver, Colorado 80202; 303-837-4791.

For Colorado, Montana, North Dakota, South Dakota, Utah and Wyoming.

San Francisco: 211 Main Street, Room 344, San Francisco, California 94105; 415-556-1186.

For Arizona, California, Guam, Hawaii and Nevada.

Seattle: 8014 Federal Office Building, 909 First Avenue, Seattle, Washington 98174; 206-442-5286.

For Alaska, Idaho, Oregon and Washington.

GOVERNORS' COMMITTEES ON EMPLOYMENT OF THE HANDICAPPED

Executive Secretary
Governor's Committee on
  Employment of the
  Handicapped
Division of Rehabilitation and
  Crippled Children
P.O. Box 11586
2129 East South Boulevard
  Montgomery, Alabama 36111

Chairman, Alaska Governor's
  Committee on Employment
  of the Handicapped
Hope Cottage
2805 Bering Street, No. 2-A
Anchorage, Alaska 99503

Executive Secretary
Arizona Governor's Committee
  on Employment of the
  Handicapped
c/o Department of Economic
  Security
Education Building
1535 West Jefferson Street,
  2nd Floor
Phoenix, Arizona 85007

Executive Secretary
Governor's Committee on
  Employment of the
  Handicapped
Employment Security Division
P.O. Box 2981
Little Rock, Arkansas 72203

Executive Secretary
Governor's Committee on
  Employment of the
  Handicapped
Employment Development
  Department
800 Capitol Mall, Room 5054
Sacramento, California 95814

Executive Director
Governor's Advisory Council
  on the Handicapped
1515 Sherman Street, 5th Floor
Denver, Colorado 80203

Executive Secretary
Governor's Committee on
  Employment of the
  Handicapped
Department of Labor Building
200 Folly Brook Boulevard
Wethersfield, Connecticut
  06109

Executive Secretary
Governor's Committee on
  Employment of the
  Handicapped
Department of Labor
1500 Shallcross Avenue
P.O. Box 1190
Wilmington, Delaware 19899

Executive Secretary
Mayor's Committee on the
  Handicapped
122 C Street N.W., Room 200
Washington, D.C. 20001

Executive Secretary
Governor's Committee on
  Employment of the
  Handicapped
Division of Employment
  Security
Department of Commerce
210 Caldwell Building
Tallahassee, Florida 32304

Executive Secretary
Governor's Committee on
  Employment of the
  Handicapped
Atlanta Rehabilitation Center
1599 Memorial Drive S.E.
Atlanta, Georgia 30317

Executive Secretary
Governor's Committee on
  Employment of the
  Handicapped
250 South King Street,
  Room 603
Honolulu, Hawaii 96813

Executive Secretary
Governor's Committee on
  Employment of the
  Handicapped
Department of Employment
P.O. Box 35
Boise, Idaho 83707

Executive Director
Governor's Committee on
  Employment of the
  Handicapped
Governor's Office of
  Manpower and Human
  Development
623 East Monroe Street,
  1st Floor
Springfield, Illinois 62701

Executive Secretary
Commission for the
  Handicapped
Indiana State Board of Health
1330 West Michigan Street
Indianapolis, Indiana 46206

Executive Secretary
Governor's Committee on
  Employment of the
  Handicapped
Grimes State Office Building
Des Moines, Iowa 50319

Executive Secretary
Governor's Committee on
  Employment of the
  Handicapped
126 South First Floor
State Office Building
Topeka, Kansas 66611

Executive Secretary
Governor's Commission on
  Employment of the
  Handicapped
600 West Cedar Street
Louisville, Kentucky 40203

Executive Secretary
Governor's Committee on
  Employment of the
  Handicapped
530 Lakeland Drive
Baton Rouge, Louisiana 70802

Executive Secretary
Governor's Committee on
  Employment of the
  Handicapped
32 Winthrop Street
Augusta, Maine 04330

Executive Secretary
Governor's Committee on
  Employment of the
  Handicapped
2100 Guilford Avenue,
  Room 201
Baltimore, Maryland 21218

Executive Secretary
Governor's Commission on
  Employment of the
  Handicapped
Charles F. Hurley Employment
  Security Building
Government Center
Boston, Massachusetts 02114

Executive Secretary
Governor's Commission on
  Employment of the
  Handicapped
Michigan Department of Labor
7150 Harris Drive
Lansing, Michigan 48926

Executive Director
Minnesota State Council for
  the Handicapped
Metro Square, 7th and Robert
  Streets
Suite 208
St. Paul, Minnesota 55101

Executive Secretary
Governor's Committee on
  Employment of the
  Handicapped
Vocational Rehabilitation
P.O. Box 1698
Jackson, Mississippi, 39205

Executive Secretary
Governor's Committee on
  Employment of the
  Handicapped
Missouri Division of
  Employment Security
P.O. Box 59
421 East Dunklin
Jefferson City, Missouri 65101

Chairman
Governor's Committee on
  Employment of the
  Handicapped
Box 1723
Helena, Montana 59601

Executive Secretary
Nebraska Governor's
  Committee for Employment
  of the Handicapped
Nebraska Department of Labor
Division of Employment
550 South 16th
Box 949600
State House Station
Lincoln, Nebraska 68509

Executive Director
Governor's Committee on
  Employment of the
  Handicapped
Kinkhead Building, Fifth Floor
505 East King Street
State Capitol Complex
Carson City, Nevada 98710

Executive Secretary
Governor's Committee on
  Employment of the
  Handicapped
6 Loudon Road
Concord, New Hampshire
  03301

Executive Secretary
Governor's Committee on
  Employment of the
  Handicapped
Division of Vocational
  Rehabilitation
Labor and Industry Building,
  Room 1005
Trenton, New Jersey 08625

Executive Secretary
Governor's Committee on
  Employment of the
  Handicapped
Technical Services,
  Employment Security
  Commission
401 Broadway, N.E.
Albuquerque, New Mexico
  87103

Chairman
Governor's Committee on
  Employment of the
  Handicapped
Human Resources Center
Albertson, New York 11507

Executive Director
North Carolina Governor's
  Council on Employment of
  the Handicapped
306 North Wilmington Street
Raleigh, North Carolina 27611

Executive Director
Governor's Committee on
  Employment of the
  Handicapped
Governor's Council on Human
  Resources
State Capitol, 13th Floor
Bismarck, North Dakota 58505

Executive Secretary
Ohio Governor's Committee on
  Employment of the
  Handicapped
4656 Heaton Road
Columbus, Ohio 43229

Executive Secretary
Governor's Committee on
    Employment of the
    Handicapped
301 Will Rogers Building
Oklahoma City, Oklahoma
    73105

Executive Secretary
Governor's Committee on
    Employment of the
    Handicapped
Oregon State Employment
    Division
875 Union Street, N.E.
Salem, Oregon 97310

Executive Secretary
Governor's Committee on
    Employment of the
    Handicapped
Bureau of Employment
    Security
Seventh and Forster Streets
Room E-161
Harrisburg, Pennsylvania 17121

Chairman
Governor's Committee on
    Employment of the
    Handicapped
Ozama 1619
Rio Piedras Heights
Puerto Rico

Executive Secretary
Governor's Committee on
    Employment of the
    Handicapped
Department of Employment
    Security
24 Mason Street
Providence, Rhode Island
    02903

Executive Secretary
Governor's Committee on
    Employment of the
    Handicapped
South Carolina Employment
    Security Commission
P.O. Box 1406
1550 Gadsen Street
Columbia, South Carolina
    29202

Executive Secretary
Governor's Advisory
    Committee on Employment
    of the Handicapped
State Office Building
Illinois Street, 2nd Floor
Pierre, South Dakota 57501

Executive Director
Governor's Committee on
    Employment of the
    Handicapped
1818 West End Building,
    Room 424
Nashville, Tennessee 37203

Executive Director
Governor's Committee on
    Employment of the
    Handicapped
Texas Employment
    Commission
15th and Congress,
    TEC Building
Austin, Texas 78778

Executive Secretary
Governor's Committee on
    Employment of the
    Handicapped
Division of Rehabilitation
    Services
250 East 500 South
Salt Lake City, Utah 84111

Executive Secretary
Governor's Committee on
  Employment of the
  Handicapped
81 River Street
Montpelier, Vermont 05602

Executive Secretary
Governor's Committee on
  Employment of the
  Handicapped
P.O. Box 1358
Richmond, Virginia 23211

Executive Secretary
Governor's Committee on
  Employment of the
  Handicapped
212 Maple Park
Olympia, Washington 98504

Executive Secretary
Governor's Committee on
  Employment of the
  Handicapped
4407 MacCorkle Avenue S.E.
Charleston, West Virginia
  25304

Executive Director
Governor's Committee for
  People with Disabilities
Park Regent Building
1 South Park Street, 4th Floor
Madison, Wisconsin 53715

Chairman
Governor's Committee for
  Employment of the
  Handicapped
611 East 16th Street
Cheyenne, Wyoming 82001

STATE AND GOVERNORS' COUNCILS AND COMMITTEES ON EMPLOYMENT OF THE HANDICAPPED

Chairperson,
Governor's Council on
  Handicapped and Gifted
Box 256
Sitka, Alaska 99835

Coordinator
Coalition for Persons with
  Disabilities
4126 South Knox Court
Denver, Colorado 80236

Coordinator
Connecticut Office of
  Protection and Advocacy for
  Handicapped and
  Developmentally Disabled
  Persons
401 Trumbull Street
Hartford, Connecticut 06103

Program Director
Vocational Rehabilitation
1309 Winewood Boulevard
Tallahassee, Florida 32301

Bureau Chief
Bureau of Vocational
  Rehabilitation
Statehouse
Boise, Idaho 83720

Coordinator
Governor's Office for IYDP
206 South 6th Street, Suite 100
Springfield, Illinois 62701

Director
Vocational Rehabilitation
510 East 12th Street
Des Moines, Iowa 50319

Coordinator
Severely Disabled Services
  Department of Education
Bureau of Rehabilitation
  Services
490 New Circle Road N.E.
Lexington, Kentucky 40505

Director
Vocational Rehabilitation
   Counseling for Blind and
   Visually Handicapped
Department of Human Services
Bureau of Rehabilitation
200 Main Street
Lewiston, Maine 04240

Commissioner
Massachusetts Rehabilitation
   Commission
1 Ashburton Place, Room 303
Boston, Massachusetts 02108

Commissioner
Massachusetts Commission for
   the Blind
1 Ashburton Place, Room 303
Boston, Massachusetts 02108

Executive Director
Committee on Handicapped
   Concerns
309 North Washington
P.O. Box 30015
Lansing, Michigan 48909

Director
Sister Kenny Institute
2727 Chicago Street
Minneapolis, Minnesota 55407

Director
Human Development
P.O. Box 139
Jackson, Mississippi 39205

Deputy Director
Department of Social and
   Rehabilitation Services
P.O. Box 5210
Helena, Montana 59601

Executive Secretary
Governor's Office
State Capitol
Santa Fe, New Mexico 87503

Director
N.Y. State Advocate for the
   Disabled
2 World Trade Center,
   Room 3712
New York, New York 10007

Executive Director
Tri-County Industries
P.O. Box 789, 123 Stratford
   Drive
Rocky Mount, North Carolina
   27801

Director
Office of Handicap Concerns
4545 North Lincoln Boulevard,
   Suite 20
Oklahoma City, Oklahoma
   73105

Administrator
Division of Vocational
   Rehabilitation
Social and Rehabilitation
   Services
40 Fountain Street
Providence, Rhode Island
   02093

Executive Director
South Carolina Developmental
   Disabled Council
1205 Pendleton Street
411 Edgar Brown Building
Columbia, South Carolina
   29201

Assistant Director
Tennessee State Planning
   Office
660 Capitol Hill Building
Nashville, Tennessee 37219

Director
Governor's Task Force for
   Handicapped Citizens
State Capitol, Room 200
Austin, Texas 78711

Office of the Governor
Department of Education
Moen Truk
Eastern Caroline Islands
Trust Territories, 96942

Executive Secretary
Vermont Developmental
   Disabilities Council
State Office Building
120 State Street
Montpelier, Vermont 05612

Commissioner
Department of Social Welfare
P.O. Box 539
St. Thomas, Virgin Islands
   00801

Secretary of Human Resources
P.O. Box 1475
Richmond, Virginia 23212

Director
Governor's Planning Reform
   Project
Office of the Governor
State Capitol Building,
   Room W-121
Charleston, West Virginia
   25305

Administrator
Division of Vocational
   Rehabilitation
131 West Wilson Street,
   9th Floor
Madison, Wisconsin 53702

Director
State Department of Health
P.O. Box 3378
Honolulu, Hawaii 96801

NOTE: In many cases the State and Governors' Councils and Committees on Employment of the Handicapped were included in Governor's Committees on the Handicapped.
Therefore, if your state is not represented in this section, refer to the Governor's Committee on the Handicapped.

APPENDIX IX

JEWISH VOCATIONAL SERVICES

National Office:
600 Pennsylvania Avenue S.E.
Washington, D.C. 20003
202-546-1970

*Jewish Vocational Service
6505 Wilshire Boulevard,
Suite 303
Los Angeles, California 90048
213-655-8910

Jewish Vocational & Career
Counseling Service
870 Market Street, Room 872
San Francisco, California
94102; 415-391-3595

B'nai B'rith Career and
Counseling Service
1640 Rhode Island Avenue
N.W.
Washington, D.C. 20036
202-857-6600

Jewish Vocational Service
318 N.W. 25th Street
Miami, Florida 33137
305-576-3220

Jewish Vocational Service of
Atlanta
1745 Peachtree Road N.W.
Atlanta, Georgia 30309
404-876-5872

*Jewish Vocational Service
1660 Sternblock Lane
Cincinnati, Ohio 45237
513-631-2400

Jewish Family and Vocational
Service
3640 Dutchmans Lane
Louisville, Kentucky 40205
502-452-6341

Associated Placement and
Guidance Bureau
5750 Park Heights Avenue
Baltimore, Maryland 21215
301-466-9200

Sinai Hospital of Baltimore
Department of Rehabilitation
Medicine
Belvedere Avenue and
Greenspring
Baltimore, Maryland 20215
301-367-7800

* Operates one or more rehabilitation workshops

These services are nonsectarian.

Jewish Vocational Service
31 New Chardon Street
Boston, Massachusetts 02114
617-723-2846

Jewish Vocational Service
4250 Woodward
Detroit, Michigan 48201
313-833-8100

Jewish Family and Children's
Service
811 LaSalle Avenue, Suite C6
Minneapolis, Minnesota
55426; 612-338-8771

Jewish Vocational Service
6715 Minnetonka Boulevard
St. Louis Park, Minnesota
55426; 612-927-6524

*Jewish Vocational Service
1608 Baltimore Avenue
Kansas City, Missouri 64108
816-GR1-2808

Jewish Family Service
775 Main Street
Buffalo, New York 14203
716-TL3-9956

*Federation Employment &
Guidance Service
114 Fifth Avenue
New York, New York 10011
212-777-4900

*Jewish Vocational Service
1 South Franklin Street
Chicago, Illinois 60606
312-FI6-6700

New York Association for
New Americans
225 Park Avenue South
New York, New York 10003
212-674-7400

National Association of
Jewish Vocational Services
225 Park Avenue South
New York, New York 10003
212-475-2400

Jewish Vocational Service
13878 Cedar Road
Cleveland, Ohio 44118
216-321-1381

*Jewish Family Service
1175 College Avenue
Columbus, Ohio 43209
614-231-1890

Jewish Employment and
Vocational Service
1624 Locust Street
Philadelphia, Pennsylvania
19103; 215-893-5900

Altro Health and
Rehabilitation Services
345 Madison Avenue
New York, New York 10017
212-684-0600

Jewish Vocational Counseling
Service
7800 Northaven Road, Suite C
Dallas, Texas 75230
214-369-4211

Jewish Vocational Service
1339 North Milwaukee Street
Milwaukee, Wisconsin 53202
414-272-1344

Jewish Vocational Service
5151 Cote St. Catherine Road
Montreal, Quebec H3W 1M6,
Canada; 514-735-3541

*Jewish Vocational Service
74 Tycos Drive
Toronto, Ontario M6B 1V9,
    Canada; 416-787-1151

*Jewish Vocational Service of
    Metropolitan New Jersey
111 Prospect Street
East Orange, New Jersey
    07017; 201-674-6330

Jewish Employment Y
    Vocational Service
1727 Locust Street
St. Louis, Missouri 63102
    314-241-3464

Jewish Vocational Service
1821 University Avenue,
    Suite S369
St. Paul, Minnesota 55104
    612-645-9377

VETERANS ADMINISTRATION REGIONAL OFFICES

474 South Court Street
Montgomery, Alabama 36104

Federal Building
U.S. Post Office and
  Courthouse
605 West Fourth Avenue
Anchorage, Alaska 99501

3225 North Central Avenue
Phoenix, Arizona 85012

1200 West 3rd Street
Little Rock, Arkansas 72201

Federal Building
11000 Wilshire Boulevard
Los Angeles, California 90024

2022 Camino Del Rio North
San Diego, California 92188

211 Main Street
San Francisco, California 94105

Denver Federal Center
Building 20
Denver, Colorado 80225

450 Main Street
Hartford, Connecticut 06103

1601 Kirkwood Highway
Wilmington, Delaware 19805

941 North Capitol Street N.E.
Washington, D.C. 20421

144 First Avenue South
St. Petersburg, Florida 33701

730 Peachtree Street N.E.
Atlanta, Georgia 30308

PJKK Federal Building
300 Ala Moana
Honolulu, Hawaii 96813

Federal Building and U.S.
  Courthouse
550 West Fort Street, Box 044
Boise, Idaho 83724

536 South Clark Street
Chicago, Illinois 60680

575 North Pennsylvania Street
Indianapolis, Indiana 46204

210 Walnut Street
Des Moines, Iowa 50309

NOTE: Address all correspondence to: Veterans Administration.

Boulevard Office Park
901 George Washington Road
Wichita, Kansas 67211

600 Federal Place
Louisville, Kentucky 40202

701 Loyola Avenue
New Orleans, Louisiana 70113

Togus, Maine 04330

Federal Building
31 Hopkins Plaza
Baltimore, Maryland 21201

John Fitzgerald Kennedy
   Federal Building
Government Center
Boston, Massachusetts 02203

Patrick V. McNamara Federal
   Building
477 Michigan Avenue
Detroit, Michigan 48226

Federal Building
Fort Snelling
St. Paul, Minnesota 55111

Southport Office Building
100 West Capitol Street
Jackson, Mississippi 39204

Federal Building
1520 Market Street
St. Louis, Missouri 63103

Fort Harrison
Montana 59636

Federal Building
100 Centennial Mall North
Lincoln, Nebraska 68508

245 East Liberty Street
Reno, Nevada 89520

Norris Cotton Federal Building
275 Chestnut Street
Manchester, New Hampshire
   03101

20 Washington Place
Newark, New Jersey 07102

Dennis Chavez Federal
   Building
U.S. Courthouse
500 Gold Avenue S.W.
Albuquerque, New Mexico
   87102

Federal Building
111 West Huron Street
Buffalo, New York 14202

252 Seventh Avenue
New York, New York 10001

Federal Building
251 North Main Street
Winston-Salem, North Carolina
   27101

Fargo, North Dakota 58102

Anthony J. Celebrezze Federal
   Building
1240 East Ninth Street
Cleveland, Ohio 44114

Federal Building
125 South Main Street
Muskogee, Oklahoma 74401

Federal Building
1220 S.W. 3rd Avenue
Portland, Oregon 97204

5000 Wissahickon Avenue
Philadelphia, Pennsylvania
   19101

1000 Liberty Avenue
Pittsburgh, Pennsylvania 15222

321 South Main Street
Providence, Rhode Island
02903

1801 Assembly Street
Columbia, South Carolina
29201

Courthouse Plaza Building
300 North Dakota Avenue
Sioux Falls, South Dakota
57102

110 Ninth Avenue South
Nashville, Tennessee 37208

2515 Murworth Drive
Houston, Texas 77054

1400 North Valley Mills Drive
Waco, Texas 76710

Federal Building
125 South State Street
Salt Lake City, Utah 84138

White River Junction,
Vermont 05001

210 Franklin Road S.W.
Roanoke, Virginia 24011

Federal Building
915 Second Avenue
Seattle, Washington 98104

640 Fourth Avenue
Huntington, West Virginia
25701

342 North Water Street
Milwaukee, Wisconsin 53202

2360 East Pershing Boulevard
Cheyenne, Wyoming 82001

Frederico Degetau Federal
Building and Courthouse
Carlos E. Chardon Avenue,
Hato Rey
San Juan, Puerto Rico 00918

COLLEGE BOARD OFFICES

New York
Program Service Officer
College-Level Examination
    Program
888 Seventh Avenue
New York, New York 10019
212-582-6210

Middle States
Director
College Board Office
1700 Market Street,
    Suite 1418
Philadelphia, Pennsylvania
19103; 215-567-6555

Midwestern
Director
College Board Office
500 Davis Street
Evanston, Illinois 60201
312-869-1840

New England
Director
College Board Office
470 Totten Pond Road
Waltham, Massachusetts
02154; 617-890-9150

Puerto Rico
Director
College Board Office
Box 1275

Hato Rey, San Juan
    Puerto Rico 00919
    809-765-5876

Southern
Director
College Board Office
17 Executive Park Drive
N.E., Suite 200
Atlanta, Georgia 30329
404-636-9465

Southwestern
Director
College Board Office
211 East Seventh Street,
    Suite 922
Austin, Texas, 78701
512-472-0231

Western
Director
College Board Office
800 Welch Road
Palo Alto, California 94304
415-321-5211

Rocky Mountains
Field Representative
College Board Office
2142 South High Street,
    Suite 23
Denver, Colorado 80210
303-777-4434

ALTERNATIVE METHODS FOR GAINING EDUCATION

High School Credit

GED Testing Service
1 Dupont Circle N.W.
Washington, D.C. 20036

Credit By Examination

CLEP College Board
Department C
888 Seventh Avenue
New York, New York 10019

ACT-PEP
1 Dupont Circle N.W.
Washington, D.C. 20036

ACT-PEP
Post Office Box 168
Iowa City, Iowa 52243

College Proficiency
   Examination Program
State Department of Education
Empire State Plaza
Albany, New York 12230

Credit for Noncollege Learning

American Council on
   Education
Office of Educational Credit
1 Dupont Circle N.W.
Washington, D.C. 20036

Credit for Experience

The Council for Advancement
of Experiential Learning
(CAEL)
American City Building,
Suite 212
Columbia, Maryland 21044

Publishes *I Can: A Tool for
Assessing Skills Acquired
Through Volunteer
Experiences*
Ramco Associates
228 East 45th Street
New York, New York
10017

Educational Testing Service
(ETS)
Princeton, New Jersey 08540

Credit for Correspondence and Independent Study

The National University
Extension Association
(NUEA), Division of
Independent Study
1 Dupont Circle N.W.,
Suite 360
Washington, D.C. 20036

National Home Study Council
1601 18th Street N.W.
Washington, D.C. 20009

EXTERNAL DEGREE PROGRAMS

Board for State Academic
  Awards
340 Capitol Avenue
Hartford, Connecticut 06115

Board of Governors B.A.
  Program
544 Iles Park Place
Springfield, Illinois 62706

Thomas A. Edison College
The New Jersey College for
  External Degrees
101 West State Street
Trenton, New Jersey 08625

Regents External Degree
  Program
Cultural Education Center
Empire State Plaza
Albany, New York 12230

The Empire State College
State University of New York
2 Union Avenue
Saratoga Springs, New York
  12866

Division of Public Affairs
University of Mid-America
Terminal Building, 10th and O
  Streets
P.O. Box 82006
Lincoln, Nebraska 68501

APPENDIX XIV

PUBLICATIONS THAT WILL HELP YOU PLAN AN EDUCATIONAL PROGRAM

Credit for What You Know
Consumer Information, Pueblo, Colorado 81009

An education fact sheet containing details of how to get high school and college credit without formal training.

A Guide to College/Career Programs for Deaf Students
Office of Demographic Studies
Gallaudet College, Kendall Green, Washington, D.C. 20002

A handy reference booklet.

A National Directory of Four-Year Colleges, Two-Year Colleges and Post-High School Training Programs for Young People with Learning Disabilities
Partners in Publishing, Box 50347, Tulsa, Oklahoma 74150

Directory includes those educational facilities that adapt curriculum and provide other services to students with perceptual disabilities.

A Guide to Post-Secondary Educational Opportunities for the Learning Disabled
Time Out to Enjoy, Inc., 113 Garfield Street, Oak Park, Illinois 60304

A directory of colleges that provide modifications for the learning disabled.

New Paths to Learning: College Education for Adults
Public Affairs Pamphlet No. 546, Public Affairs Committee, Inc., 381 Park Avenue South, New York, New York 10016

A sprightly written pamphlet packed with information on alternative ways of getting a higher education.

Higher Education Can Be Part of Your Future
Closer Look, Box 1492, Washington, D.C. 20013

Handbook for Blind College Students
National Federation of the Blind, 218 Randolph Hotel Building, Des Moines, Iowa 50309

> Booklet lists regional libraries, machine lending agencies, braille presses, print book enlargement agencies and magazines available through the Library of Congress.

The College Guide for Students with Disabilities
ABT Publications, 55 Wheeler Street, Cambridge, Massachusetts 02138

> This directory is geared primarily for students with physical, hearing and visual impairments. It provides information on services, policies and accessibility features of colleges and universities throughout the United States, and also lists federal and state agencies that provide support for disabled individuals, sources to contact for financial aid and where to write for helpful learning aids, materials and publications.

Directory of Accredited Home Study Schools
National Home Study Council, 1601 18th Street N.W., Washington, D.C. 20009

> This directory gives a partial list of subjects offered, along with names and addresses of accredited home study schools. If you don't find the subject or school of your particular interest in your area, write to them. They may have instituted a program since the writing of the directory.

Library of Congress
Washington, D.C. 20542

> Books for the blind and physically handicapped. The Library of Congress provides library service to the blind and physically handicapped residents of the United States and its territories. The program provides talking books, books in braille and the talking book machines. There are 56 regional libraries and 104 subregional libraries in the United States with a collection of approximately 29,000 titles in recorded and braille form. There are also over 30,000 music scores, textbooks and instructional materials in braille, large type and recorded form.

Guide to the Section 504 Self-Evaluation
National Association of College and University Business Officers
1 Dupont Circle, Suite 510, Washington, D.C. 20036

> Self-evaluation for compliance with Section 504.

ORGANIZATIONS IN COLLEGES AND UNIVERSITIES SERVING DISABLED STUDENTS

People United for Self Help
The University of Alabama
P.O. Box 1943
University, Alabama 35486
205-348-5306

P.I.L.M.
Pima Community College
2202 West Anklom Road
Tucson, Arizona 85709
602-884-6666

ARC Handicapped Student
  Union
American River College
4700 College Oak Drive
Sacramento, California 95841
916-484-8382

Cabrillo Inconvenienced
  Students' Association
Cabrillo College
6500 Soquel Drive
Aptos, California 95003
408-475-6000, x293

Disabled Students on Campus
c/o Dean of Student Affairs
California State University
Fresno, California 93740
209-487-2741

Self-Help Rap & Referral
  Center
California State University
Adm. 579
Hayward, California 94542
415-881-3657

Disabled Students' Coalition
California State University
18111 Nordhoff
Northridge, California 91324
213-885-2869

Handicapped Students'
  Association
Building TWX-West
6000 J Street
California State University
Sacramento, California 95819
916-454-6955

NOTE: This is a partial listing. If you do not find the college or university of your choice listed here, write to that institution requesting information on organizations serving disabled students.

Disabled Students' Union
California State University
1600 Holloway Avenue,
 PSY 103C
San Francisco, California 94132
415-469-1546

Disabled Students' Coalition
Disabled Student Services
 Offices
California State College-
 Sonoma
1801 East Cotati Avenue,
 Stevenson 2011-A
Rohnert Park, California 94928
707-795-2356

Disabled Students' Union
ENABLER program
City College of San Francisco
B-402, Special Education
50 Phelan Avenue
San Francisco, California 94112
415-587-7272, x560

Handicapped Programs and
 Services
College of the Desert
45-500 Monterey Avenue
Palm Desert, California 92260
714-346-8041, x261

Learning Center Community
 Club
College of San Mateo
1700 West Hillsdale Boulevard
San Mateo, California 94402
415-574-6437

Roosevelt Center for Disabled
 Students
Cypress College
9200 Valley View
Cypress, California 90630
714-826-2220

Disabled Students'
 Involvement Club
East Los Angeles College
5357 East Brooklyn Avenue
Los Angeles, California 90022
213-263-7261, x452

Disabled Students' Program
El Camino College
16007 Crenshaw Boulevard
Via Torrance, California 90506
213-532-3670, x278

Disabled Club
Fresno City College
1101 East University Avenue
Fresno, California 93741
209-442-4600, x355

Handicapped Services Office
Grossmont Community College
8800 Grossmont College
 Boulevard
El Cajon, California 92020
714-465-1700, x402

Rotaract Club
Los Angeles Valley College
5800 Fulton Avenue
Van Nuys, California 91401
213-781-8542

Handicapped on the Move
Merced College
Student Activities Office
3600 M Street
Merced, California 95340
209-723-4321, x255

Enabler Services
Modesto Junior College
MM108-435 College Avenue
Modesto, California 95350
209-524-1451, x237

MPC Physically Impaired Club
Monterey Peninsula College
Student Activities Office
980 Fremont
Monterey, California 93940
408-649-1150, x233

Handicapped Students' Center
Orange Coast College
2701 Fairview Road
Costa Mesa, California 92626
714-556-5807

Lancer Deaf Students' Club
Pasadena City College
1570 East Colorado Boulevard
Pasadena, California 91106
213-578-7261

Disabled Student Services
San Diego State University
San Diego, California 92182
714-286-6473

DELTACAPS
San Joaquin Delta College
5151 Pacific Avenue
Stockton, California 95207
209-478-2011, x288

Disabled Students' Union
San Jose State University
c/o Student Activities Office
San Jose, California 95192
408-277-2188

Disabled Student Center
Santa Ana Community College
17th and Bristol
Santa Ana, California 92706
714-835-3000, x418

Disabled Students' Union
University of California
1780 Spruce Street
Berkeley, California 94709
415-849-3098

Services to Handicapped
    Students
University of California
1st Floor-Silo
Davis, California 95616
916-752-3184

Disabled Students' Union
Special Services
University of California
Riverside, California 92502
714-787-4538

College & Community
    Handicapped Advancement
    Society
Victor Valley College
18422 Bear Valley Road
Victorville, California 92392
714-245-4271, x249

Center for the Physically
    Handicapped
Community College of Denver
1001 East 62nd Avenue
Denver, Colorado 80216
303-287-3311, x241

Handicapped Student
    Organization
University of Colorado
1100-14th Street, Room 3A
Denver, Colorado 80202
303-892-1117, x449

Office of Special Student
  Services
University of Connecticut
Box U-174
Storrs, Connecticut 06268
203-486-2020

Counselor for the Handicapped
University of Hartford
200 Bloomfield Avenue
West Hartford, Connecticut
  06450
203-243-4689

Student Services Specialist
Federal City College
425 Second Street N.W.,
  Rm 1115
Washington, D.C. 20001
202-727-2987

Handicapped College Student
  Committee
Office of Student Development
  (F-209)
Sante Fe Community College
3000 N.W. 83 Street
Gainesville, Florida
904-377-5161

Office of Disabled Student
  Services
Florida State University
101 Bryan Hall
Tallahassee, Florida 32306
904-644-6013

Handicapped Student Services
Florida Technological
  University
P.O. Box 26272
Orlando, Florida 32816
305-275-2371

People Helping People
University of Miami
P.O. Box 8809
Coral Gables, Florida 33121
305-284-3930

Advisory Committee on
  Handicapped Students
University of South Florida
Ctr. 217
Tampa, Florida 33620
813-974-3180

Veterans Association
Augusta College
Augusta, Georgia 30904
404-828-2896

Advisory Board for
  Handicapped Students
Georgia State University
University Plaza
Atlanta, Georgia 30303
404-658-2206

Office to Promote
  Independence of Disabled
  Students
University of Georgia
Activities Center-Memorial Hall
Athens, Georgia 30602
404-542-1559

Komo Mai
University of Hawaii-Leeward
  Community College
96-045 Ala Ike
Pearl City, Hawaii 96782
808-455-0288

Handicapped Student
  Association
Idaho State University
Campus Box 8345
Pocatello, Idaho 83209
208-236-0211

Director, Rehabilitation
Counselor Education
University of Idaho
College of Education
Moscow, Idaho 83843
208-885-7079

College Youth Against
Disabilities
Northeastern Illinois University
5500 North St. Louis Avenue
Chicago, Illinois 60625
312-583-4050, x355 or 356

Disabled Student Association
Southern Illinois University at
Edwards
Students Activities Office
Edwardsville, Illinois 62025
618-692-2686

Delta Sigma Omicron
University of Illinois
Oak Street at Stadium Drive
Champaign, Illinois 61820
217-333-4600

DSIA (Disabled Students in
Action)
Ball State University
St. B-13
Muncie, Indiana 47306
317-285-4572

Vice-President's Committee for
the Handicapped
Indiana University
316 North Jordan
Bloomington, Indiana 47401
812-337-4902

Handicapped Student
Association
Indiana University-Purdue
University
1201 East 38th Street, KB 54
Indianapolis, Indiana 46205
317-264-2540

Vocational Rehabilitation
Counselor
Community College (Des
Moines Area)
2006 Ankeny Boulevard
Ankeny, Iowa 50021
515-964-0651

Project Chess
Drake University
1320 - 24th Street
Des Moines, Iowa 50311
515-271-3889

PUSH
Ad Hoc Committee for Barrier
Removal
University of Iowa
Student Activities Center
Iowa City, Iowa 52240
319-353-2121

Handicapped Student
Association
Emporia Kansas State College
1200 Commercial Street
Emporia, Kansas 66801
316-343-1200

Human Relations Center
University of Kentucky
Room 5, Alumni Gym
Lexington, Kentucky 40506
606-258-2751

College Association of the Deaf
  Delgado Chapter
Delgado Junior College
615 City Park Avenue
New Orleans, Louisiana 70119
504-486-7393, x346, 347

BEACON
University of Southwestern
  Louisiana
USL Box 3970
Lafayette, Louisiana 70501
318-233-3850, x207

B.U. Committee of
  Handicapped Students
Boston University
George Sherman, Room 411
775 Commonwealth Avenue
Boston, Massachusetts 02115
617-353-3658

Access Boston
Phillips Brooks House
Harvard University
Cambridge, Massachusetts
  02138
617-495-2703 (home phone - R.
  Lazar)

Handicapped Student Center
University of Massachusetts
Boston Harbor Campus
Dorchester, Massachusetts
  02125
617-287-1900, x2922

Special Services Program for
  Handicapped Students
Michigan State University
Room W409
East Lansing, Michigan 48824
517-353-9642

Dean of Students' Office
Northern Michigan University
Marquette, Michigan 49855
906-227-2132

Disabled Student Services
University of Michigan
4119 Michigan Union
530 South State Street
Ann Arbor, Michigan 48104
313-763-3000

Educational Rehabilitation
  Services
Wayne State University
450 Mackenzie Hall
Detroit, Michigan 48202
313-577-2424

Committee for the
  Handicapped
University of Minnesota
  Technical College
Waseca, Minnesota 56093
507-835-1000

Broncos
Southwest Minnesota State
  College
Marshall, Minnesota 56258
507-537-6296

The H.E.A.R.T. Club
Pennsylvania Valley
  Community College
3201 Southwest Trafficway
Kansas City, Missouri 64111
816-756-2800

Association of Handicapped
  Students
Southwest Missouri State
  University
Springfield, Missouri 65802
816-831-1561, x258

Council of Handicapped
  Students
University of Missouri-
  Columbia
1201 Paquin, Apt. 312
Columbia, Missouri 65201
314-882-2121

Disabled Students' Committee
Eastern Montana College
Billings, Montana 59101
406-657-2307

Programs for the Handicapped
Clark County Community
  College
3200 East Cheyenne Avenue
North Las Vegas, Nevada
  89030
702-643-6060

Kean College
BS-A14
Brynwood Gardens
Old Bridge, New Jersey 08857
201-679-3385

Take a Second Look
Middlesex County College
Center IV
Edison, New Jersey 08817
201-548-6000, x377

Disabled on Campus (DOC)
University of New Mexico
1608 Roma N.E.
Albuquerque, New Mexico
  87106
505-242-6868

CAMPIS (Coalition to Assist
  Medically and Physically
  Inconvenienced Students)
Bronx Community College
West 181 Street and University
  Avenue
Bronx, New York 10453
212-320-6450

Student Organization for Every
  Disability United for
  Progress
Brooklyn College—CUNY
Bedford Avenue and Avenue H
Brooklyn, New York 11210
212-780-5102/5103

Handicapped Students
  Organization
Canisius College
2001 Main Street
Buffalo, New York 14208
716-833-7000, x232, 233

Student Government
  Organization
Hostos Community College—
  CUNY
475 Grand Concourse
Bronx, New York 10451
212-933-8000, x325

Disabled Students'
  Organization
Hunter College—CUNY
695 Park Avenue, Room 100
New York, New York 10021
212-360-2475

CUNY Committee for the
  Disabled
City University of New York
96 Schermerhorn Street,
  Room 1103
Brooklyn, New York 11201
212-831-0333

So-Fed-Up (Student
Organization for Every
Disability United for
Progress)
Queensborough Community
College—CUNY
Student Activities Office
Bayside, New York 11364
212-631-6446

Coordinator, Programs for the
Handicapped
Dutchess Community College
Pendell Road
Poughkeepsie, New York 12601
914-471-4500

Living Library for the Blind
Fordham University
c/o Director of Student
Activities
125 Keating Hall
Bronx, New York 10458
212-220-1190/933-2233,
x722/610

PUSH (People United for
Support of Handicapped);
PHED (Program for Higher
Education of Disabled)
Hofstra University
1000 Fulton Avenue, Student
Center
Hempstead, New York 11550
516-560-3221

Determined Students for the
Disabled
New York University
Box 47, Loeb Student Center
566 Laguardia Place
New York, New York 10012
212-598-3223

Committee to Assist Physically
Disabled Students
Queens College
I Building, Rooms 119A & B
Flushing, New York 11367
212-520-8094

NTID Student Congress
Rochester Institute of
Technology
Rochester, New York 14623
716-464-2508

Disabled Student Information
& Service Center
State University of New
York—Binghamton
Easter Seal Office—University
Union
B13 SUNY, Binghamton
Binghamton, New York 13901
607-798-3197

Community Action Corps
State University of New
York—Buffalo
3435 Main Street
Buffalo, New York 14214
716-831-4542

Disabled Students'
Organization
Staten Island Community
College
715 Ocean Terrace
Staten Island, New York 10301
212-390-7872

Alpha Phi Omega
Syracuse University
Archbold Gymnasium
Syracuse, New York 13210
315-423-3433

Ad Hoc Committee to
  University Planning Office &
  Office of Student Affairs
University of North Carolina at
  Chapel Hill
Ol Steele Building
Chapel Hill, North Carolina
  27514
919-933-2107

Everybody's Organization
University of North Dakota
University Station
Grand Forks, North Dakota
701-777-2011

Students for Mobility
Kent State University
c/o Human Relations
  Department
Kent, Ohio 44242
216-672-3391/672-7955

Wheelchair Sports Club &
  Architectural Barrier
  Committee
c/o Handicapped Student
  Services
Wright State University
Dayton, Ohio 45430
513-873-2141

Helping Service Club
East Central University
Horace Mann Building,
  Room 222
Ada, Oklahoma 74820
405-332-8000, x3100

SHARE
Oklahoma State University
Rehabilitative Services
Quanset 2, Room 22
Stillwater, Oklahoma 74074
405-372-1995

Committee of Handicapped
  Students
c/o Counseling Center, Ad S
  Building
Oregon State University
Corvallis, Oregon 97331
503-754-2131

CRIP/Associated Students of
  Portland State University
Portland State University
P.O. Box 751
Portland, Oregon 97207
503-229-4456

Coordinator, Programs for
  Disabled Students
Community College of
  Philadelphia
34 South 11th Street
Philadelphia, Pennsylvania
  19107
215-569-3680

Disabled Student Union
Montgomery County
  Community College
340 Dekalb Pike
Blue Bell, Pennsylvania 19422
642-6000, x441

Coordinator, Center for
  Disabled Students
Poley Library, Room 320
13th and Berks Streets
Philadelphia, Pennsylvania
  19122
215-787-1280

Chairman, Students'
  Committee for Disabled
University of Pennsylvania
1438 Thornberry Road
Wyncote, Pennsylvania 19095
215-886-6080

URI Committee for the
Handicapped
University of Rhode Island
Administrative Building,
Room 109
Kingston, Rhode Island 02881
401-792-2933

"Not Psyched Out" Club
Eastfield College
Mesquite, Texas 75149
214-746-3180

Handicapped Students'
Division of Student Association
Texas Tech University
University Center
Lubbock, Texas 79409
806-742-4114

Organization for the Handicapped
University of Houston
2132 Colquitt
Houston, Texas 77006
713-522-4247

M.I.G.H.T. (Mobility Impaired
Grappling Hurdles Together)
University of Texas at Austin
c/o Student Activities Office
Texas Union South
Austin, Texas 78712
512-471-1201

Student Services
University of Utah
160 Union Bldg.
Salt Lake City, Utah 84112
801-581-5020

Richmond Center for the Deaf
J. Sargeant Reynolds
Community College
P.O. Box 6935
Richmond, Virginia 23230
807-770-8432

Barrier Breakers
Fort Stellacoom Community
College
Coordinator, Physically
Handicapped
9401 Farwest Drive S.W.
P.O. Box 99
Tacoma, Washington 98499
206-552-3181

ASVW Disabled Student
Commission
Room 207 HUB, PK-10
University of Washington
Seattle, Washington 98195
206-543-2100

Physically Impaired Student
Services Program
Office of Dean of Students
Washington State University
Pullman, Washington 00163
509-335-4531

Student Government
Committee for the
Handicapped
Student Affairs Office
Milwaukee Area Technical
College
Milwaukee, Wisconsin 53203
414-278-6227

Associate Dean of Students
University of Wisconsin-Parkside
Kenosha, Wisconsin 53140
414-553-2342

Students for an Accessible
Society
Education/Psychology Building,
Room 2039
University of Wisconsin
Whitewater, Wisconsin 53190
414-472-4711